Airbnb Marketing

A Guide for Beginners How to Start and Market Airbnb Rental House Business

By Emily Bennett

The trademarks that are used are without any consent, and the publication of the trademark is without permission or backing by the trademark owner. All trademarks and brands within this book are for clarifying purposes only and are owned by the owners themselves, not affiliated with this document.

Table of Content

CHAPTER 1: INTRODUCTION TO AIRBNB.........................7

1.1 History of Airbnb...7

1.2 Current Goals and Objectives.....................................11

1.3 Advantages And Disadvantages of Airbnb...................14

1.4 Performance...18

1.5 Swot Analysis...19

CHAPTER 2: THINGS WE CAN LEARN FROM AIRBNB'S
MARKETING STRATEGY.......................................24

2.1 Brand Partnership..24

2.2 Influencers...27

2.3 Taking Risk...30

2.4 Quality Imagery..33

2.5 Building A Community...35

2.6 Digital Marketing Strategies.......................................36

CHAPTER 3: COMPARISON BETWEEN AIRBNB AND
THE PRIVATE RENTAL SECTOR..........................40

3.1 The Differences in the Sharing Economy......................42

3.2 Accommodation Seekers...46

3.3 Facilities and Length of Stay.......................................50

3.4 Reputation and Trust..54

3.5 Prices 58

CHAPTER 4: GETTING INTO AIRBNB AS A BEGINNER AND MANAGING YOUR DAILY HOLIDAY RENT 62

4.1 Set Up A Profile 63

4.2 Check Out the Previous Reviews 66

4.3 Check the Location..69

4.4 Communication Is Key 71

4.5 Prepare Your Property 74

4.6 Competition Analysis..77

4.7 Create the Perfect Listing 78

CHAPTER 5: WHAT IS AIRBNB SEO? 82

5.1 Create and Measure Your Optimization Goals 83

5.2 Study the City and Top Leaders 88

5.3 Optimize Your Current Listing..............................92

5.4 Promote Your Listing...96

CHAPTER 6: HOW AIRBNB BENEFITS COMMUNITIES?
....99

6.1 Economics of The Sharing Economy 99

6.2 A Platform Built on The Community Trust...........105

6.3 The Future Regulatory Environment 107

CONCLUSION 110

REFERENCES 112

Chapter 1: Introduction to Airbnb

Travel, as an industry, has been evolving dramatically. In recent years, sharing economies have become more popular, giving rise to companies like Airbnb that utilize sharing economies to create an online marketplace for the exchange of private products and services. Sharing economies have complex dynamics in how they form relationships between market participants. The lines between customer and seller become blurred, and trust has become an increasingly important factor as this trend continues to grow. In the travel industry, in particular, Airbnb has been utilizing this unique structure to create a new type of experience for its customers. This book aims to give an in-depth review of Airbnb, its competitors, and the travel industry as a whole. An analysis of the firm and production delivered to determine whether the vacation rental industry itself is favorable. Next, it examines the core strengths and competencies that Airbnb has developed to succeed in the industry. Four key market segments identified as business travelers, low-budget culture seekers, event-goers, and group/family travelers. Low-budget culture seekers isolated as the ideal segment based on their potential to further Airbnb's overall goals. Lastly, this book will inspect how Airbnb fills the necessity of its entire section in a method that is meaningful and differentiated from its competitors.

1.1 History of Airbnb

Small-term rentals have been around for quite some hour, but with the notion of home-sharing, it was Airbnb, which strengthened the short rental space. Airbnb's history is the success story of an innovative startup, demonstrating how online lodging revolutionized by a pair of housemates with an idea.

While Airbnb has been privately owned and operated independently throughout its existence, similar to Booking.com's history, Airbnb created from a simple design made possible through the internet.

The original plan for Airbnb was born out of desperation when Brian Chesky and Joe Gebbia, co-founders and housemates, we're struggling to pay their rent and came up with an innovative way to make some extra money. The two designers had found that a local conference on industrial design resulted in a full booking of the nearby hotels in San Francisco, so they put down three air mattresses and provided a bed and some breakfast for any designers who needed a place to stay during the conference. Chesky and Gebbia created their site named airbedandbreakfast.com instead of using Craigslist, which seemed "too impersonal" to advertise their room.

Chesky and Gebbia realized that they had stumbled across an idea worth creating, after hosting three designers for $80 a night during the seminar. They quickly enlisted the help of computer science graduate Nathan Blecharczyk and former housemate of Gebbia to help them construct a more robust website and forum to offer online home-sharing between users. The Democratic National Convention in Denver, as the site finished in the summer of 2008, had caused a shortage of hotel rooms. The three founders targeted the region and ended up having a successful launch with hundreds of listings, yet they still didn't benefit from the project and needed money.

With the 2008 U.S. election catching the attention of people, Gebbia and Chesky decided to put their sketch and marketing skills to work, designing custom-made cereal boxes for Obama-O and Cap'n Mccain. We sold these cereal boxes of "limited edition" for $40 each and ended up raising $30,000 to put into the operations of the company.

While the personalized cereal boxes helped keep the company going, it wasn't long before venture capitalists started taking notice and investing in the company. At the beginning of 2009, Paul Graham invested $20,000 and had the company join his famous startup accelerator, Combinator. It allowed Airbnb to spend several months developing its product, while at the same time attracting investment from other venture capitalists. The company shortened its name from Air Bed & Breakfast to its current name Airbnb in March 2009 and began overgrowing in part thanks to Sequoia Capital's $600,000 investment. Many investments quickly started to roll in, and Airbnb had become a profitable, internationally operating company in the span of a few years.

Part of the immense success in Airbnb's history has been the constructive versatility encountered by the business is facing challenges. When a host's home was trashed and ransacked by her Airbnb guests in the summer of 2011, the company immediately acknowledged their failures and set up a security policy to help protect hosts in the event guests were damaging property or stealing property during their stay. While the "Host Guarantee" from Airbnb covered property damage and fraud worth $500,000 initially, it doubled to a million dollars in 2012. Airbnb has shown a similar kind of constructive approach in reacting and collaborating primarily with cities to ensure that their hosts support the law on short-term rentals. That said, the company has also embroiled itself in a variety of legal battles with cities and governments, which it claims to control or limit short-term rentals wrongly.

Airbnb agreed to update its website and logo in 2014, with "belonging" is the central concept behind the redesign. They switched from colder corporate blues to a hotter, more solid red peach color, and a complete redesign of the company logo came along with it.

Chesky and Gebbia agreed that the original logo was born quickly and automatically, with its newer logo being a mixture of people, locations, love, and Airbnb's "A." The Belo, the name of Airbnb's logo, marks a critical point in Airbnb's history and the growth of the company. Since the launch of the Bélo, Airbnb has begun offering its customers more than just accommodation. For anyone interested in booking them, Airbnb Experiences is a platform for people to run workshops, city tours, and different unique city experiences. Chesky has recently revealed plans for Airbnb to start creating travel content such as movies and T.V. series, taking the lodging giant into the entertainment industry. With their hiring of the former CEO of Virgin America airlines Fred Reid, Airbnb has made moves in the travel business. Although Chesky said the organization was not interested in creating its airline, in the past, he clearly stated his intention to revolutionize the travel industry, with the addition of Reid bringing the dream of Chesky closer to reality.

Just as fascinating are the plans of Airbnb with their recent purchase of ten Rockefeller Centre's tales, so the company is planning what appears to be a hotel-like service of dedicated Airbnb spaces. While Marriott International and other hotel companies are beginning to look into the business of home-sharing, Airbnb is already growing, expanding, and developing its services. While Airbnb's past is already notable, it is clear that the company plans to expand on its legacy. Airbnb has disrupted the hotel and hospitality industries as the company prepares for what expected to be a historic launch of the IPO by the end of 2019.

Airbnb is based in more than 191 countries and is expanding globally. They have managed to set up operations in Cuba and other countries where their legitimacy might be in doubt. By doing so, they've built a market that suits travelers, including big spenders, penny pincers, and everyone in between.

1.2 Current Goals and Objectives

The main objective of Airbnb is to increase its market share and its consumer income by employing added services. It demonstrated by Airbnb expanding its services outside of accommodation and building a lively tourist community within cities while encouraging the more significant adaptation of goods on the global market. Talking about his New York dream, Brian Chesky said, "We envision a more accessible New York, which even more people can afford to travel to, where extra space in people's homes Not going to waste, and where millions of visitors patronize small businesses in the neighborhood in all five districts It will be a community where tens of thousands of jobs will generate for people like photographers, tour guides and chefs to sustain it vibrant new ecosystem.-Brian "Chesky   For its newest product, Airbnb has now focused on promoting development-" Experiences." "Experiences" provide unique experiences that allow guests to experience local cultures authentically. "Experiences" are more complicated than rentals, which require more quality control and management.

For this reason, Airbnb has started to set up its city-by-city activities and experiences. In each region, Airbnb management reviews and approves "experience" plan in advance, rather than enabling guests to list them openly as they did with rental accommodations. In a Fortune interview, Brian Chesky clarified the complexities of listing events as opposed to homes. with Experiences, starting with a controlled marketplace was more relevant because, with a home, it must be at least good.

There was no existing quality bar with experiences because it was so fresh.

As we did pilots, some lessons were fantastic; some were not even experiences. "Another aim that Airbnb had been working on was product adaptation to promote travel around the world. Today, a primary focus is broader markets that differ significantly from the U.S. and European markets. China, in particular, is a popular destination for travel with enormous potential for development. Individualistic societies, such as the United States, are more vocal and less risk-averse, making their participants more likely to adapt to cooperative economies.

In contrast, China has a collectivistic culture, which means that long-standing social bonds are significant. The Chinese are far less likely to trust strangers or embrace short-term relationships, which said that the Airbnb model needed considerable adaptation before it could succeed in the Chinese market. For Airbnb's nearly 4 million listings, only 80,000 are currently in China. In March, Airbnb announced plans to rebrand itself as "Aibiying" in China, which roughly translates into "welcoming one another with love. "It also announced plans to partner with the influential Chinese social app WeChat and help the Chinese payment method Alipay to promote greater brand trust in Chinese consumption.

Airbnb has implemented a massive expansion program. The road map positions 1 billion annual visitors on the network by 2028 over the next ten years. The deals are shared spaces, private rooms, or you can rent the whole building, but now the aim is to include holiday homes, exclusive areas, beds and breakfasts, and boutiques.

The company initially targeted the lonely traveler but noticed that consumers had different needs, like places to cook, want extra space, or explorers searching for an offbeat course. Airbnb has established Collections to meet these needs, which include Airbnb for Family and Work.

The goal is to encourage clients to book group stays, weddings, honeymoons, group getaways, and dinner parties. This feature set to launch later this year.

Additionally, Airbnb Plus provided by the company. For quality and comfort, these homes individually tested. The project involves 2,000 households spread across 13 different cities — this feature intended for clients seeking a guaranteed quality experience.

If that's not enough, then with Luxury Retreats, the company takes things one step further. As of last year, Airbnb has made an acquisition that developed into Beyond, providing the finest of custom-designed trips to rolled out this spring.

We're left to wonder about one thing, with all the updates to the app. The company has changed how they deal with diversity and inclusion on the website so that their new slogan is really "for everyone."? They're saying, yes.

"The goal in the rollout of all these different elements was to prove that we have a coherent approach to making Airbnb for everyone," said Policy Development Manager Margaret Richardson. "My first mission at Airbnb was the attempts to fight discrimination.

I began outside and then joined the company in the middle of efforts to address that anti-discrimination was part of the community pledge we made, and we had a 97 percent acceptance rate." "What we have seen is that among our employees, we have been able to diversify the team we have in Airbnb and continue our dedication to diversity for hosts and guests alike. "We continue to invest in the anti-discrimination component of our platform, we have brand alliances with organizations such as the NAACP and the American Human and Rights Leadership Conference, and we are looking to be both in the technology world and in the future. "We exceeded that, but we still realize this is not enough, "Janaye Ingram, National Partnerships director, told Black Enterprise. "There's a lot of opportunities and a lot of things we're looking at to do better to ensure we're building a professional talent pool that can come in and do both technical and non-technical positions." "This year, we're collaborating with a lot of groups as the Bed and Breakfast starts, and the Boutique Hotel launch takes place," said Cammy Houser, Traditional. "I've been into some fascinating conversations about helping underrepresented minority owners, and we're trying to think deeply about how Airbnb might help these businesses thrive."

1.3 Advantages And Disadvantages of Airbnb

The Advantages:

There are many advantages to using Airbnb for hosts and guests alike. Airbnb provides an opportunity primarily to connect guests with the right kind of hosts. If you want to rent a palace or beach house in the country of your choice, there are several options listed by Airbnb.

Hosts and guests can have a meeting before the dates of their stay. You, as the host, know precisely how many people are coming and what they need. As a visitor, you'll know what to expect in terms of rent rates and facilities. Guests can even inquire about the host questions about and how to get to key tourist spots in the city. Hosts can provide valuable details about the area, e.g., key attractions, tidal conditions, air temperature, transportation facilities, equipment to carry, etc. The quality of the service is also more personalized, particularly if the traveler books a room in the host's house, just like in a bed and breakfast setting.

And rental prices do, of course, continue to be much lower compared to standard hotel rates. You can rent a whole three-bedroom house for a fraction of what three rooms or a suite in a hotel would cost. You can be confident, with the Airbnb guarantee that your accommodation will be ready at the right time.

Airbnb's Advantages Large Range Airbnb hosts list several different types of properties— single rooms, suite rooms, condos, moored yachts, houseboats, whole homes, even a castle — on the Airbnb website.

Free Listings: Hosts need not pay for listing their properties. Listings can include written explanations, captioned images, and a user profile where potential guests can get to know the hosts a little bit.

Hosts Can Set Your Price: It is up to each host to decide how much to charge for each night, week, or month.

Customizable Searches: Guests can look at the Airbnb database–not only by date and location, but also by price, property type, amenities, and the host language. We can also add keywords such as "next to the Louvre" to narrow their search even further.

Additional Products: Airbnb has extended its services in recent years to include restaurants and experiences. In addition to a list of available hotels for the dates they plan to travel, a list of activities, such as classes and sightseeing, provided by local Airbnb hosts will show to people searching by location. Airbnb hosts comments also included on restaurant lists.

Protections for Visitors and Hosts: Airbnb keeps the guest's payment 24 hours after check-in before transferring the funds to the host as security for visitors.

To hosts, the Airbnb Host Guarantee policy "protects the protected property in the rare event of guest injury, in qualifying countries, to up to $1,000,000 in damages."

The Dis Advantages:

Along with the benefits, the use of Airbnb rentals often poses certain dangers and disadvantages. The chance of property damage or loss is present for the host, whether deliberate or not. In one area, especially at night, there are incidents of security breaches for tourists depending on the status of peacekeeping.

Once you close a deal with a host, guests may not consider their backgrounds. Those, however, represent only a fraction of the overall host-guest experience, and most Airbnb arrangements for both parties have been smooth and satisfying. However, there were cases of fraud. People act as hosts but are not the real owners of the property.

Such negative encounters and other threats can be minimized by using the security features of Airbnb, such as Verified I.D.s, Profiles, Secure Payment System, and the Host Guarantee, as well as by reading reviews of guests who have leased the property that interest you. Hosts should speak to their insurance companies about how to protect guests from harm to their property.

Furthermore, hosts and guests alike should be mindful of local laws which may limit or even ban property rentals, in particular zoning or administrative codes. For example, some cities may allow hosts to buy licenses or permits. Guests should also be mindful that they could also hold liable while renting property without understanding that doing so is illegal. Hosts also need to pay income tax on rentals in individual states and countries.

What you glimpse may not be what you get to book accommodation with Airbnb isn't like booking a room with a significant lodge chain, where you have reasonable assurance that the property will be as advertised. Individual hosts make their lists, and some may be more honest than others. Nonetheless, past visitors also post comments on their encounters, which can provide a more objective view. Potential damage Probably the most significant danger to hosts is damage to their properties. Most stays go without incident. There are reports that hundreds of party-goers were trashing entire houses when the Airbnb owners thought they were renting to a peaceful couple. Airbnb's Host Guarantee policy, mentioned above, offers some coverage but may not cover everything like cash, rare artwork, jewelry, and pets. Hosts whose homes are affected may also face substantial inconvenience.

Additional Charges: Airbnb imposes several additional charges as do hotels and other providers of accommodation, of course. In addition to the accommodation fee, visitors pay a guest service charge of 0 percent to 20 percent to cover customer support and other services provided by Airbnb. Prices appear in the currency chosen by the customer, provided Airbnb sponsors it. Banks or issuers of credit cards can charge additional fees, if applicable.

And while rentals are free, Airbnb charges for hosting a service fee of at least 3 percent for each booking, for covering the transaction processing expense.

Taxes: A value-added tax (VAT) that apply to both hosts and guests from the European Union, Switzerland, and Norway. And the hosts may be subject to rental income taxes depending on their venue. Airbnb collects user details from hosts to assist with U.S. tax compliance so they can give an account of their earnings each year through 1099 and 1042 forms.

It Isn't Legal Everywhere Before listing their property on Airbnb. Would-be hosts need to review their local zoning regulations to make sure their properties rented legally. Hosts may also expect to get individual licenses or permits.

1.4 Performance

Airbnb is a privately owned enterprise. For this reason, all performance numbers informed estimates which are measured using external source information. According to the Bloomberg Report for Airbnb's 3rd Quarter in 2017, revenue amounted to approximately $1 billion. In 2016, market share ranged from 1% in Washington DC to 3.9% in Greater London. The global market share reported at approximately 2.7%. It would be a.2% improvement from its estimated 2015 market share of the worldwide holiday rental industry.

The exact net profit margin for Airbnb on the rent mentioned here is undisclosed. It charges a three percent fee for each listing that covers the cost of listing on its platform. It also pays a six percent-12 percent fee per booking for each guest, which can be called their estimated net profit margin.

That presumption, however, cannot compensate for the costs of running and setting up tours on its website, because Airbnb is still planning the feature and it is uncertain how it will affect the net profit. Moreover, as a fast-growing company with an expected 40% to 50% growth in listings per year, Airbnb rentals could make up 3.6% to 4.3% of the inventory by 2020.95 Market share, about 2.7% in 2017, which reflects an improvement of 0.2% between 2016 and 2017. The figures shown below are:

Current Market Share 2017: [($1bn)/($35.9bn)] * 100= 2.7%.

Market share growth 2016-2017: [current market share (2.7%)] -(previous market share [$900 million]/ [35.9 billion] * 100= 2.5%) = 2.7%-2.5%= 2.2% growth.

1.5 Swot Analysis

Strength:

Airbnb was the first-holiday rental company to integrate its business model into a sharing economy. Being the industry's first mover helped Airbnb to get a head-start on the scale, which is one of its competitive advantages. It also gained a lot of recognition as a first mover, both positive and negative, which led to a high brand awareness level. Airbnb is a very familiar brand, the majority of people living in the countries where Airbnb operates are aware of it and of the primary services it offers. Airbnb has spread to international markets, which tremendous untapped potential for growth. The site provides plenty of customer interaction sources, which is essential for the model as it depends on consumer feedback and reviews. Airbnb uses a star-system to determine hosts and guest rankings. Finally, additional services, such as location photographers, and their innovative "Experiences," are a significant strength that Airbnb provides to the users over competitors.

Well-established Brand-Airbnb is a well-established brand with an excellent public reputation where it operates. The business model of the company allows the company to compete with low prices as opposed to hotels and visitors.

Brand Expansion–Airbnb has extended its offerings beyond its core lodging, intending to create an end-to-end travel platform. It also extended its operations to allow guests to book activities with guides such as guided tours, cooking classes, and meetings.

A Cheaper Hotels Alternative–Airbnb is seen as a cheaper alternative to other resorts and hotels. The services' rates are sustainable, location dependent. Customers can search around, and they can pick the venue that suits their budget.

Global Recognition-Airbnb has recognized globally, seeing many users, including hosts and guests.

Airbnb Plus–Airbnb Plus is a unique feature Airbnb has offered, introduced in 2018. The different options under Airbnb Plus provide additional services such as those found in hotels, from essential to luxury listings.

Airbnb Collections–Airbnb Collections, released during 2018 by Airbnb, offers homes that are suitable for any particular occasion. Airbnb for jobs, Airbnb for families and homes for dinner parties, celebrations, and weddings are among the various options under the Airbnb sets. Airbnb for work provides different resources for companies that handle several employee's travels related to the job.

Social Media Presence–Airbnb has its presence on many social media platforms to gain maximum consumer exposure.

Excellent customer service–Airbnb offers 24/7 customer service to the product, which is one of the company's main strengths. If they make the customers happy, other people are there for them.

Weakness - One of Airbnb's key drawbacks is that it relies heavily on tourists. The plan of staying in a stranger's home leads many to think back to the age-old saying:' stranger risk.' Although most guests have fun, problem-free stays using Airbnb, there have been instances where hosts have taken advantage of the booking process's almost anonymous nature. Guests found a spy camera in the house in 2017, which they rented through Airbnb. It is just one example, and it highlights a significant weakness within Airbnb-relying on its hosts and the need to curate a level of trust that is appropriate for their guests and hosts. Airbnb is also dependent on its customers to fill their portfolio with attractive, affordable rents. If Airbnb were to endure any significant string of incidents linked to its brand, rebuilding trust with both consumers and homeowners listed on its site would be extremely difficult.

Violations of laws and regulations–Airbnb faces problems in violating various rules and regulations relating to housing.

Poor Hosts-Being - a poor host, can damage the reputation of the company. If the host does not meet the Airbnb guidelines in any situation, they may face the consequences. If poor ratings and social media criticism arise, it affects the income of the organization in the current business world.

Easy to Replicate Business Model - Airbnb business model is easy to copy, and for its popularity, it is a considerable weakness.

The Guest Review System – Objectivity, Airbnb has developed a review system that allows guests and hosts to rate each other after their stay completed. Hosts and guests are unable to see feedback after both gave a score.

Criticized for higher prices–Airbnb criticized for having created a high price for the stay. Rental prices in a few places have risen because Airbnb takes their properties off the long-term rental market, and instead gets higher rental rates for short-term accommodation.

Opportunities:

As discussed before, one of the primary goals for Airbnb is development. In this region, Airbnb has tremendous opportunities because its model applies worldwide. Several reports have suggested that Airbnb is considering adding additional services such as personal chefs and choices for travel. As many of Airbnb's direct competitors also provide these services, this is an excellent opportunity.

Additionally, Airbnb exceptionally well placed for collaboration opportunities, which could make product adaptation considerably easier for new markets, which is what we are beginning to see in China. Furthermore, most of Airbnb's current customers are people ages 25-44. To include older and younger users, Airbnb may widen its business.

Expand into Emerging Markets–Airbnb could expand to less competitive emerging markets. That offers an immense business opportunity.

Expanding its offering–Airbnb will broaden the mix of goods and deals. That will allow them to serve the customers better. It can extend its offering, for example, by providing travel guides, car rentals, etc.

Mobile App Usage–As mobile app usage increases, Airbnb has introduced a mobile app that will make it easier for hosts and guests to connect.

Low Price and Personal Touch-The The low price and personal touch of Airbnb allowed them to gain exposure and more revenue.

Threats:

New entrants are among the significant risks facing Airbnb. As the sharing economy continues to get bigger, increasing numbers of businesses are attempting to replicate or create similar models to Airbnb. The increasing competition is generating a further challenge in the form of price wars. As more firms enter the market, Airbnb might tempt to compete as a cheap option, but it is a fast race to the bottom, and these kinds of price wars can be harmful to a company. The last, and perhaps most significant, challenge facing Airbnb is, as a rivalry, larger companies. Like TripAdvisor's Flip Key and other similar rivals, Airbnb does not have a large parent company's backing. It cannot borrow directly and hides its intentions from its competitors. The prospect of adding restrictions constitutes a threat to Airbnb's future.

Laws and Regulations–In each country Airbnb services are available in approximately 192 countries. Every state and every nation have to respect its rules and regulations. The firm will rely carefully on guests and hosts to allow them to comply with local laws.

Lawsuits–The firm already faces some lawsuits and fines in places like New York, Florida, etc. around the world. The Barcelona authorities have fined the Airbnb company for violating the tourism laws with around 30.000 Euros. The New York Authority has even prosecuted Airbnb for operating unauthorized hotels.

Rivals–Airbnb has many competitors, such as tripping.com, and many more. That can give the Airbnb business a hard time.

Chapter 2: Things We Can Learn from Airbnb's Marketing Strategy

Airbnb provides lodging in more than 100,000 cities and 191 countries worldwide. More than 180 million people have found accommodation through the Airbnb web site since its inception in August 2008 and until May 2019. He was able to take a leading position in the visitor services industry almost immediately. Airbnb is well leading the competition when it comes to mixing available with extraordinary.

Growth for Airbnb has been fast, mainly due to its unorthodox, inspiring, and creative marketing strategies. It is not the result of lavish marketing budgets, but the result of hard work, in-depth market analysis, and creative ingenuity. When it comes to marketing, Airbnb has plenty of marketing strategies to teach everyone!

Following are the Airbnb marketing strategies:

2.1 Brand Partnership

A partnership with a client is a mutual agreement between two or more entities or organizations. Through these alliances, companies help each other maximize brand exposure, expand into new markets, and add value to the products/services they offer.

Airbnb has shown us countless times that collaborations can cause a lot of noise and severe impact. Airbnb's successful relationship involves KLM Airlines, the Waterstones UK bookstores chain, and even the French government. Impressive!

The heart of the collaboration is creating a special deal for both brands' customers — the value proposition you can only provide with a partnering brand.

For instance, the contest created with KLM in which the winners could spend a free night in luxury "Aircraft apartment." It was a night in the Halloween, with the French government, which helped raise the image of a less popular French tourist destination.

It starts with your brand to distinguish your Airbnb company from the competition in a crowded market place. The development of a brand is the cornerstone of an effective marketing campaign for Airbnb, as it builds long-term trust and loyalty. Getting your brand for your vacation rental company also makes telling the guests of your property more comfortable. When they prepared to book with you once more, they will find you quicker.

Come up with a name for your business and create a logo to establish your brand. Use your brand name and symbol on all your social media accounts and holiday rental platforms to streamline your Airbnb digital marketing strategy. Fifty-two percent of travelers look for recommendations on social media when planning a trip, according to the latest data. Surprisingly, 42 percent of Facebook posts are travel tales, making Facebook the perfect place to advertise your holiday rental business.

To incorporate Facebook into your Airbnb marketing strategy, start by creating a Facebook business page for your properties. Including posting about your wealth, you can also use your business page on Facebook to share useful traveler content like tips & suggestions. Eventually, to increase interaction with your Facebook page and draw more fans, you can also run a paid Facebook Advertising campaign. Facebook can tell you directly on your business page how much exposure a paid ad campaign will get you and how much it costs to promote your message.

While Facebook can provide some stellar results for your Airbnb marketing strategy, Instagram is where the action is right now. Especially if you want to meet the younger audience, this can come in handy. More than 500 million people use Instagram daily.

Instagram is also a highly visual platform ideally suited for sharing photos and videos. It is where all of your assets can highlight in their complete glory. Follow Instagram's best marketing practices by making sure you look professional with your photos and videos.

Finally, invest in your properties in professional photography. Even learning how to use smartphone apps to improve your Lightroom, Afterlight, etc. images is a good idea. By using apps, you can create great content for your own Instagram account, and save a fair amount of money on your own.

YouTube is not only the most popular video website but also behind Google's second-largest internet search engine. YouTube has a billion users worldwide, and its users are increasing their consumption of video content.

The creation of a YouTube channel is a great way to help you personalize your brand. Your marketing strategy for YouTube Airbnb should focus on creating videos that feature your properties, as well as helpful tips for travelers. Try creating engaging content that will help travelers get to know your area better. Make videos about the top attractions your area offers, for example, and what makes it a must-see venue to visit.

The quality of your Airbnb marketing strategy needs to bring real value to travelers. You would appreciate insider tips and feedback from someone who knows the area exceptionally well.

Videos with titles like "Top 5 Beaches to Discover" or "Top 10 Things to Do in Your City" have the best chances to get your audience famous. The more popular your content is, the higher the YouTube search results will rank as well. YouTube's Airbnb marketing strategy should also focus on building up your subscribers.

2.2 Influencers

Influencer marketing's main objectives are to boost brand support, increase brand awareness, reach new target markets, improve sales conversion, manage credibility, accelerate the generation of leads, improve customer satisfaction. Because 84% of millennials and 73% of non-millennials prefer to plan a trip based on vacation photos or social media posts from someone else, influencer marketing cannot distinguish from the marketing strategy of Airbnb.

Through partnering with some of the greatest names in the entertainment industry, Airbnb has been able to effectively create brand awareness, increase its visibility to mass audiences on social platforms, including Instagram, where 700 million users are active monthly. In turn, this will help to redefine Airbnb as a premium brand name in terms of customer understanding, rather than just a cheap accommodation provider.

Airbnb abused the incredible effect of the influencers they collaborated with since they assumed that staying in fascinating Airbnb properties is synonymous with their lifestyles. As part of their strategy, Airbnb organized its sponsorship program to get coverage from both the social media community and news in tandem with significant popular events.

For Mariah Carey, their first influencer campaign began in 2015. At that moment, with more than 6 million followers on Instagram, Carey tagged Airbnb in her tweet, with 45,000 likes then got. By collaborating with Lady Gaga in a campaign in 2017, Airbnb exposed its brand name to 27 million Lady Gaga followers on Instagram, creating enormous opportunities for potential customers to approach Airbnb. Influencer marketing approach has significantly contributed to Airbnb's tremendous credit growth in the last few years

It's a well-known fact that working with popular influencers is an effective Digital Marketing Strategy for Airbnb to boost your rental business. YouTube, there are a lot of travel bloggers that can help you gain exposure for your company.

Nonetheless, a relationship with an influencer only yields success if you first do the following Identify the Right Influencer–You should know your audience inside and out and consider the audience of the influencer to make sure the influencer fits well. Consider the age of the followers of the influencer and their future desires.

Set Specific Goals and Objectives–You need to decide in advance what aspects you want to encourage in your vacation rental business. And, more importantly, how you gage your ad campaign's progress.

Defining Terms and Conditions with a Contract-what will the influencer receive in return for your business promotion? What are the minimum requirements which must be met by the influencer to account for their efforts? How are you going to stop your marketing campaign if the collaboration doesn't go as intended? Make sure a contract is all in writing.

One of the most time-consuming aspects of your Airbnb marketing strategy is likely to be finding influencers to promote your vacation rental business. Make sure you plan for the best results with care.

Over the past ten years, Airbnb has developed into a $38 billion business that gives the world's top hotel chains fierce competition. Their business model has disrupted the hospitality industry in a bid to become a household name and outperform its competition. One aspect that has contributed to Airbnb's meteoric rise is its Instagram-specific influencer marketing campaign.

It's commendable how Airbnb has leveraged Instagram by partnering with some of the world's most celebrities to gain massive exposure to the brand. Today, with influencer marketing, we will delve into Airbnb's journey and gain insight into this approach. Instagram, as a marketing platform with more than 1 billion active monthly users, is a great choice to spread brand awareness. According to Airbnb's Rachel Haley Global Connections Strategy Lead, celebrity influencers are helping to showcase the desirable lifestyle and position the brand as a luxury alternative to hotels. Influencer marketing's organic existence highlights the authentic experience of visiting a city rather than a superficial tourist experience. When you live with a resident like a regular, you'll immerse yourself in the community and expertise every taste that the city has to offer. Influencer marketing indeed correlates the lifestyle of a town with the brand Airbnb.

Consideration of how they dominated the global market is essential. In 2011, Airbnb began expanding overseas and is now operating in 17 countries. Why did Airbnb do it when so many American companies struggled to translate their popularity to the overseas market?

Chalk it up to the use of local influencers to boost awareness of the brand through several smartly run campaigns. The point is to strike the right balance between a global strategy and domestic application.

The procedure is to collaborate with prominent influencers in a particular location with a specific area of expertise.

Airbnb launched an influencer content series in 2015, in which experts shared local experiences that people in their city should try. Airbnb partnered across channels with local bloggers and content creators to give tips on things to try out in their respective cities. In 2015, Airbnb collaborated on a Night At campaign with a K-Pop artist G-Dragon to help its expansion into South Korea. There was a contest, of which the winner could spend two nights in the artist's recording studio. It was gaining a lot of attention from social media and a rise in Airbnb registration in Korea. In 2016, the Airbnb London office designed an exclusive townhouse where visitors could experience local music and food. They were offering an opportunity to experience "the real London" A team of 25 influencers has been tapped on social media to spread awareness about the case. Millions of people came to know about this, and over the next four days, 1400 people visited the townhouse. Wherever Airbnb goes, they worked with local influencers to let them tell the audience about the company and its fantastic service. It is an intelligent strategy that combines global and regional elements for maximum impact. Local influencers made the people feel a primarily foreign brand, inspiring confidence and reliability as local. They walk their talk, all credit to Airbnb.

2.3 Taking Risk

As a host, you are well aware that some Airbnb risks are associated with renting your property to strangers. While there are threats that can handle, you must know precisely what you are facing so that you can effectively minimize them.

When renting guests to Airbnb, you essentially allow strangers to stay at your house.

While you may feel that during your pre-check-in meetings, you've built up some study, you have no idea how things really will turn out until the guests arrive.

Liability as a result of actions or accidents taken by your guest while the guest is on your premises is just one of the significant risks that the host has to find ways to mitigate. A visitor can get hurt, harm your property, or even cause neighbors injury. As the property owner, you are going to be on the hook for these things.

Instead of thinking you will be able to weasel your way out of a civil lawsuit, make sure you have the correct Airbnb liability insurance policy in place before you list your property on Airbnb at all. Not only will it help to minimize your out-of-pocket expenses, but it can also protect you from personal liability. Renting to settlers is one of the Airbnb risks that all hosts are worried about, regardless of how many properties they have in their portfolios. In some areas, in just a few weeks, squatters will exercise their right to live on your property as tenants, and they are often pretty hard to get rid of them.

Unintentional guests end up selling to invaders and then face lengthy processes of eviction, which cost thousands of legal fees. The hosts, meanwhile, are also losing chances to rent to potential Airbnb guests. Squatters also frequently cause property damage, ensuring that the Airbnb host will also be on the hook for those costs.

To prevent renting to squatters, hosts will attempt to avoid long-term rentals where the line Relationships between short-term rental guests and tenants are unclear unless a rental agreement is in effect. Airbnb hosts should as well be on the lookout for visitors who don't have a definite departure time or want to renegotiate checkout dates after they've arrived. One of the significant issues faced by all Airbnb hosts is a continually changing regulatory environment.

In response to Airbnb's growing popularity, many cities around the world are looking to place more significant restrictions on short-term property rentals through the enactment of new zoning regulations and rental legislation.

As a result, a time could come when holiday rental services such as Airbnb would prohibit in your area. However, even if Airbnb is not banned, governments can end up making compliance costs so high that making healthy profits from your company becomes almost impossible for you.

To avoid the risk of running an unlawful Airbnb company or being forced out of the market, all Airbnb hosts must remain on top of regulatory changes that impact short-term vacation rentals and the hotel sector. Hosts should never depend on Airbnb directly to provide them with these details because it is likely too late to reduce the damage to your business once the information is made available via Airbnb.

By becoming more involved in your local government, you will have the opportunity to share your thoughts or vote on issues impacting Airbnb guests until new proposals become law. As an Airbnb host, you know that when it comes to booking cancellations, Airbnb has the final say. If Airbnb guest protests, even after the check-in date has passed, Airbnb can decide to cancel their reservation, and return all the money to the guest.

It can happen irrespective of the cancelation policy Airbnb has provided in your listing. Additionally, Airbnb doesn't even have first to contact you to discuss the cancelation.

Airbnb may also determine to stop payment on a reservation, even after the guest has checked out. You will also not reimbursed for the money you have already shelled out to provide the guests with the lodging and services agreed upon during their stay.

Although canceled bookings like this are generally rare, at some stage, you can expect to lose money on a reservation. Therefore, as part of your Airbnb management strategy, you need to account for unforeseen cancelations that result in lost revenue so that you don't end up in red. In areas where Airbnb usage is significant, Airbnb may have an impact on the overall value of properties on that market. Airbnb can potentially adversely affect the cost for properties where most of the units rented out on Airbnb.

Some of Airbnb's opponents argue that Airbnb is harming the community aspect of living in a neighborhood as transient, short-term tenants do not maintain properties as well as locals. It's also a given that security might be lax in a building where Airbnb is allowed to accommodate traveling guests.

Sadly, real estate prices in your market could begin to reflect these negative assumptions, pushing your property's price down. While this doesn't always happen, one of the Airbnb issues that hosts should know about if they idea to buy and sell properties to grow their Airbnb businesses is the potential for lower property values.

2.4 Quality Imagery

Airbnb appreciates the significance of high-quality images and thus offers a free professional photo for all its guests to maintain a particular model and style on social media.

We spend more money on production than on marketing, as we realize that better content can draw more considerable attention ever. Travel lovers use Airbnb because they feel lovely by what they see on the website's beautiful photos.

Airbnb understands the importance of high-quality images, and that's why they offer free professional photography to all of their hosts to maintain continuity across their media.

We still spend more money on development than on marketing, as we realize that there will always be more attention to better quality content. Travel lovers use Airbnb because they feel excellent by the beautiful pictures; they see on the Airbnb website.

Take some time to arrange everything before taking photos of your room, as if you were preparing to welcome your first visit. All your images should represent your room and help set expectations of your guests before they book.

Here are some tips for taking high-quality pictures: add a variety of images: to help visitors understand what it's like to visit in your space, take photos of your listing inside, outside, and neighborhood.

Resolution matters: Take at least 1024x 683px images. If in doubt, it is easier to have a bigger picture.

Take your pictures in landscape format: All the images in the search results displayed in landscape, so vertical pictures will not show your space.

Set the scene: Clean and remove the clutter to make your space look inviting and spacious.

During the day, take photos: Open the blinds and turn on the lights to make your space brighter.

Highlight unique amenities: Visitors love to stay in character spaces, so watch out for details such as a fireplace, or treehouse.

Showcase accessibility features: Emphasize quality features that are helpful to visitors with limited mobility, for example, large doorways, step-free floors, and grab rails.

2.5 Building A Community

Airbnb is more than just a source of P2P accommodation; it's a culture, by building trust between users, they have built up their community. They foster regular communication, detailed profiles, and robust review. The contribution is genuinely phenomenal.

They also streamlined the booking process by creating a community. Once users first sign up, they need to build their profile, but after that, it's as easy as entering their payment details.

This one-step process is miles ahead of anything conventional hoteliers offer and part of the reason people continue to come back to Airbnb. It offers high-quality accommodation in the best places, at reasonable prices, which can book in just a few easy steps.

It is also the experiential authenticity that makes Airbnb such a popular culture. With extensive local knowledge of the best eateries, transport links and hidden gems, hosts go out of their way to make their visitors happy.

Airbnb is a huge supporter of bringing people together from all walks of life, and they have worked firm to build a community around their brand. We rely on the hosting community to acquire hosts and have evolved through word-of-mouth referrals since the start., this has continued to be an integral part of their business, even as they developed into a multi-million-dollar company. Today, through community discussions, gamification, content marketing, and their fantastic user experience, the community remains at the heart of the Airbnb brand! It keeps travelers returning for more, even if other choices may be cheaper or more convenient.

Airbnb is more than a mere provider of accommodation; it is a travel lovers' culture. The site takes pride in building confidence and creating personal connections with other users.

Communication is regular between visitors and hosts, which helps to address any issues or answer any questions that travelers might have. All users are required to create images and details of their profiles.

The online community of Airbnb is a network for non-guest hosts that has existed for more than five years and has been through many changes and approaches during this period.

The group is based on the Lithium platform, using the most available Lithium modules. It ensures that the network helps hosts to ask questions, exchange tips and tricks, communicate with other hosts, propose ideas, build and host meetup groups, and engage in home-sharing clubs with each other. The group also uses translation to appeal to different languages rather than separate sites.

Main challenges for a mature, highly active community such as Airbnb usually include handling high activity levels, being highly responsive to members' questions, and ensuring that members engage in actions that drive the brand's real value.

Issues can also arise with the importance of an online community. The larger the group is, the more it needs the squad. As the team's size grows, so does the temptation to cut the budget when the community's value cannot be proven.

2.6 Digital Marketing Strategies

Airbnb's real success is its transcended pure brand and has become a lifestyle. Create that particular moment when the guest says: "Wow, this is much better than the hotel." They create a customer for life at that moment.

Now We Will discuss Airbnb's digital marketing strategies and how it is essential in Airbnb marketing strategy.

I dug a little and found that this "other" exposure for holiday rentals in Germany is mostly due to ratings, which makes sense because ratings constitute a significant part of the business strategy for online vacation rentals, particularly in a peer-to-peer marketplace. Of course, Airbnb uses the rating system just like the others for their rental listings, but they also make sure the Trustpilot.com reviews appear in their AdWords listings. As I looked at the other top 5 group domains, it didn't seem to be part of their digital marketing strategy.

We are talking about Airbnb's handling of listings as a form of carefully curated content in an Airbnb marketing plan. The most desirable spaces on Airbnb's website are ranked higher in the search results of the site. At the same time, listings with lower ratings or material of lower quality, in general, are more difficult to find due to a robust algorithm and employees who curate and have the best content.

Returning to the visual stimulation concept, Ayer also mentions how Airbnb provided the mutually beneficial service of professional photographs of the spaces listed on the site and guidelines for user-generated images. The visuals, therefore, offer better content, and the areas are becoming more appealing for users looking for a place to live. It's a win scenario for Airbnb as its digital marketing strategy optimizes its search engine listings, enabling the cream to increase to the top, which in turn keeps Google's search engine's users interested.

Another factor affecting a website's SEO is the size of the site, too. Airbnb has nearly 3 million pages indexed in Google, while the other top 5 domains, except for fewo-direkt.de, don't even make it past 2 million.

While Airbnb.de has considerably more pages, users create content on the site, which creates a tradeoff: the company doesn't have to spend time and money creating content, but they don't have to manage over the content of the listings either. It means that although Airbnb.de might want to be organically visible in Germany's top-head keywords, due to the content that dominates the website, the pages might not need optimized on such keywords. I left my favorite digital marketing strategy, last used by Airbnb. Airbnb had been quite resourceful when they started. At first, Airbnb found that they had to partner with two digital marketing companies to get enough customers. Google is the place to be for any e-commerce website, but Craig's List can be useful for holiday rentals, particularly for a peer-to-peer company. That unusual move allowed Airbnb to get the hosts and customers needed to give them a good head start in their business. Why did those giants interact with them?

Since people were already using Craig's List to post short-term housing ads, Airbnb decided to allow people to share their Airbnb posts on Craig's List as well, driving more traffic to both the listing of users and the Airbnb web site.

Such digital marketing tactics have been worth mentioning as Airbnb is doing quite well in online search despite their competition. Internationally, Airbnb opposes active players, which developed in their respective markets. The online marketplace should establish a robust digital marketing plan to serve the public, though with a splash of insight from the competitive landscape and a few smart men and women thinking outside the box. Airbnb appears to be a great example of a company that has begun to struggle as any start-up might and has risen to the top by understanding its market and taking advantage of opportunities.

Long-tail keywords work well, but highly sought after, and competitive head generic keywords push market shares, particularly in vacation rentals. These are some essential and useful things we can learn in Airbnb marketing strategies.

Chapter 3: Comparison Between Airbnb And the Private Rental Sector

Over the lifetime, technological developments have made it easier for people to connect, e.g., mobile phones, the world wide web. That promotes the sharing of information. The sharing economy has grown in tandem with shifted attitudes towards consumption, increasing concerns about climate change, and a desire for social inclusion through local and collective use. The sharing economy, described as' a peer-to-peer practice of receiving, giving, or exchanging access to goods and services, organized through community-based online services,' has become an important industry estimated at $15 billion in global revenue. It also expected to continue to grow to $335 billion by 2025, which means there is considerable potential for growth in the sharing economy. The sharing economy rise will have enormous social effects and is, therefore, relevant to policymakers as well as implementers. A critical type of sharing is the sharing of accommodation with its most famous Airbnb marketplace.

Airbnb founded in the year 2008. More than 60 million visitors have already equipped with lodging since then. Airbnb is a peer-to-peer market place that matches people who have room to rent to people seeking a place to stay in more than 192 countries. It allows tourists to rent out their room, studio, apartment, and house, thus offering a unique travel experience. Because of Airbnb, visitors can stay at the individuals' homes. It allows them to meet the owner, see how the owner lives, and feel the different culture of the place in which they reside. At first, to generate an extra income for tourists, Airbnb was a great alternative for hotels and homeowners.

Nevertheless, it also has an essential impact on other markets due to the tremendous rise in Airbnb lodging worldwide. Across the Netherlands, Airbnb entered. However, the number of Airbnb's in Amsterdam, currently over 11,300 lists, accounts for 45 percent of all accommodations in the Netherlands.

This paper discusses Airbnb's potential impact on the Amsterdam private lease market. Airbnb is continuing to increase in Amsterdam, and this city's municipality is one of the first cities to announce a cooperative effort with Airbnb to provide a concentrated solution for the private holiday rental market. Many rules came forth out of this joint effort. The municipality of Amsterdam is trying to cope with the rapid increase in Airbnb accommodation in the city by imposing these regulations. It is essential because, according to research, the growing amount of Airbnb's could be the reason why Amsterdam's house prices are rising. The residential community is widespread, which could help homeowners in Amsterdam, but could also be detrimental to potential home seekers, and the availability of rooms for students to rent.

In this chapter, I will highlight the impact on the city of Amsterdam of the increase within Airbnb rentals and to what degree the legislation will affect social welfare. Currently, Airbnb's expansion is impacting Amsterdam's hotel industry and the private rental market. My theory is that the city will ultimately benefit from the accommodation sharing network, thanks to legislation introduced by the municipality of Amsterdam. I will concentrate on research on the sharing economy as a whole in the next segment and will address the similarities and differences between Airbnb, the hotel industry, and the private rental sector.

I will then concentrate on Airbnb's effect on Amsterdam's private rental sector and how it affects the various actors.

I will give insights into how the regulations guide Airbnb in the subsequent section. Finally, I will explain my findings, present my conclusions, discuss limitations, and provide ideas for further investigation.

3.1 The Differences in the Sharing Economy

The sharing economy distinctions and similarities between Airbnb and the private rental sector I will first explain in this section what the sharing economy is and how it affects different markets. Second, I'm going to look at the similarities and differences between those markets.

The sharing economy does not have a uniform definition, but the sharing economy idea is to reduce transaction costs and increase convenience. Rachel Botsman defines new platforms generated through the sharing economy as powered by network technologies that allow the sharing and exchanging of assets from spaces to car skills in ways and on a scale never before possible.' She argues that these new platforms enable assets previously inaccessible or not conveniently available to become widely accessible. Pushmann refers to the sharing economy as a mechanism for separating physical goods or services so that ownership can be shared with others, allowing for a new phenomenon such as' collaborative consumption,' where access to products and expertise is more important than property. Hamariet describes three driving forces behind resource sharing. Second, for many goods and services, consumer behavior changes from possession to sharing. Second, technological advances make it easier for consumers to connect via online social networks and electronic markets. And thirdly, by creating mobile devices and online systems, the use of shared goods and services is made more convenient.

Because of these drivers, platforms such as Airbnb can be successful in the economy of today.

Technological advances also empowered people to connect, which also opened the possibility of exchanging goods and services. Airbnb has developed an accommodation sharing system through the creation of a website, where individuals are the consumer.

It is because of these innovations that individuals can now circumvent traditional intermediaries and redefine classical business partnerships. Through investing in these new markets, people are better able to conduct economic transactions without traditional corporate intervention. The change allows networks to bring people together and thus create demand. Gansky describes two business models that cover all platform styles. The first is called the' Full Mesh' model, where the company's assets are leased and make a profit. The second is called the' Own-to-Mesh' model, where, for example, Airbnb, third parties create a network to link individuals to goods and services.

In this latter model, Botsman describes three groups. The first category is' product management systems' where it's a service that allows the exchange of multiple products or privately-owned products to be shared or leased peer-to-peer.' In this category, ownership of the asset is not essential. The concept is the' redistribution markets' where pre-owned goods sold to someone who no longer needs or uses them. Botsman claims this is another option to "reduce, reuse, recycle, restore" widely used. A third category is' the habits of collaboration.' In this group, people with similar interests, for example, time and skills, come together to share and exchange intangible assets. All three categories can be related to Airbnb. Privately owned rooms shared between residents and visitors, it is possible to redistribute this to tourists if anyone has a spare bedroom that is not used, even for a short period. Airbnb guests can also relate to their hosts because they are open to meeting new people and building confidence.

Airbnb is an excellent tourist solution, and thus acts as a good alternative for hotels.

Therefore, it influences the hotel industry. However, due to its popularity and enormous worldwide expansion, we can also see some developments in other markets, such as the private rental market. Airbnb is a rival in the hotel industry, which offers housing that might also be ideal for the private rental market. To assess Airbnb's influence, I will consider its similarities and differences with the hotel industry and with the private rental market on four different characteristics: accommodation seekers, accommodation facilities and length of stay, reputation and confidence, and price.

Over the past few years, the Airbnb team has completed its economic impact studies and drawn some reassuring conclusions about the positive impact that Airbnb has to offer. For starters, one of the significant driving forces motivating travelers to take advantage of Airbnb is that persons want to experience a place as if they were one of the locals. As a result, Airbnb guests are staying and spending in many different neighborhoods throughout the area. These are neighborhoods that many times before the dawn of Airbnb wouldn't have attracted many tourists. On top of that, these Airbnb guests payout more than twice the amount usually paid by daily visitors!

And, concerning the outcry about Airbnb rentals killing the hotel industry, this isn't exactly the case. More than 70 percent of Airbnb listings are, in fact, properties that based outside the districts of the major hotels, according to data collected by Airbnb.

Nowadays, people focused on enjoying a more authentic travel experience, and this is something that hotels cannot offer almost as good as the economy of sharing Airbnb.

What sets apart Airbnb hosts from your receptionist at one of the big brand-name hotels is that Airbnb hosts are excellent at sharing tips on the elusive, undiscovered gems the city has to offer. It means that the Airbnb sharing economy encourages tourists to support the small local businesses and not just the main attractiveness that appears on the front cover of glossy magazines and big billboards.

The Airbnb sharing economy is not only helping the local small businesses. The grim reality is that the economic outlook in many countries is somber. There's a lot of people struggling to earn enough money to survive without getting debt. While hundreds of Airbnb hosts are generating additional revenue for the growth of the Airbnb Sharing Economy, half of all Airbnb hosts collected by Airbnb admit that they cannot stay home for financial gain. Airbnb Sharing Economy.

Apart from these financial advantages, individual hosts have built invaluable entrepreneurial skills thanks to the Airbnb sharing economy, while also increasing their awareness of customer service and marketing. Many of these Airbnb hosts have no prior experience in the hospitality industry, and these newly acquired skills and knowledge motivate them to enter any industry as these skills are essential in virtually every sector.

For some hosts, it's more than just supplementing their revenue. The economy of Airbnb sharing has created a new group of talented entrepreneurs called "rental entrepreneurs." Yes, according to information gathered by Learn Airbnb, at least more than 70 American Airbnb hosts raise more than $1 million a year just by renting out their assets.

Interestingly, the Airbnb sharing economy has had a positive impact on conventional property management. Airbnb may have been a community where individual property owners used to rent out their properties.

Still, nowadays, property management agencies are also using the platform to list their thousands of listings. These firms create jobs for hundreds of people, and so the Airbnb sharing economy has also helped sustain job creation in this sector.

It is clear that, by benefiting both local businesses and residents, the Airbnb sharing economy has helped countless local economies from around the globe. And not just financially!

Without it, our lives would have been far more impoverished too. The Airbnb community promotes cultural awareness, understanding, and tolerance, and now more than ever, this is priceless.

3.2 Accommodation Seekers

Citizens have various reasons for looking for accommodation. Hotels and Airbnb provide accommodation for tourists and business people looking just for short term accommodation. A convenient place to stay, where they can relax and unwind. Where hotels see a diverse group of guests; however, the people who book Airbnb accommodation are typically younger. At 45, over 64 percent said they used a home-sharing service, while only 23 to 29 percent of people who are 45 or older used it. A positive correlation also appears to exist between the experience with peer-to-peer travel and income, but not between using a home-sharing service and pay.

Nevertheless, it is not only the number of tourists using Airbnb increasing but also the number of businessmen using the service.

Airbnb has created a portion that is only intended for business travelers and offers full rooms and apartments. At this moment, competing with the hotel industry on a larger scale but also having an impact on the private leasing market.

The private rental market offers houses and apartments for home and rental seekers, who are looking for a place to live, so these groups are looking for long term accommodation. They need to be acquainted with the community because they will spend a significantly longer time in their new housing than the visitors and businesses mentioned above.

With an immovable market in which over 80 percent of home seekers leverage online search tools, it was only time before an application such as Airbnb was launched, with a unique twist, to address a particular market for hosting seekers.

Did you ever wish you could rent part of your home comfort to people seeking accommodation at any time, even for just one night? If yes, then you would be happy with Airbnb's system, which connects individuals who are willing to rent part of their homes to travelers and hosting seekers. The company is estimated at over $25.5 billion so far and is increasingly popular among homeowners and tourists — including business travelers searching for executive accommodation in luxurious homes.

So how does that impact the residential real estate market as a whole? Is Airbnb the lucky for the realtors? What are its valuables and demerits?

A full assessment of its impacts, it is essential first to understand what it is and how it ultimately links all involved parties. According to the company's website, Airbnb provides "a trustworthy online platform for people to view, discover, and book unique lodging around the world." Even with property listings from more than 192 countries, the company is still planning to expand and stabilize.

Apart from helping homeowners to monetize part of their homes, Airbnb is a favorite because it allows individuals to list their properties at no charge.

The platform is versatile enough to fit a wide variety of features including condos, townhouses, houseboats, yachts, camping cabins, single rooms, mansions, and more.

Each night can help you decide how comfortable you want to be, and the system will provide you with information such as photos, descriptions, titles, and titles that you can effectively use to advertise your property. They can do it. It is particularly critical, as 83 percent of home seekers generally favor recruiting property owners who include photos in their listings.

Airbnb is not advertising websites where accommodation seekers can easily search realtors and property owners for phone numbers. They must first register and create profiles before they can continue with booking reservations. The platform only allows visitors to book tickets to protect homeowners after completing forms with their information and then paying through one of the major credit cards or one of the secure online payment systems Google Wallet and PayPal offered. An additional 6-12 percent guest service fee charged as a host guarantee and customer service charge in addition to the rent fee. Moreover, the actual sums are only deducted from a traveler's account once the homeowner has verified the reservation.

Ironically, Airbnb, the fees are not issued to the homeowners automatically deducted from the accounts of the guests. Airbnb only releases payments to homeowners 24 hours after check-in as a measure to protect travelers through the available payout options that include paper checks only for Canada and the United States, Western Union, Payoneer, Paypal, International Bank Transfer and Automated Clearing House. Airbnb makes some money off homeowners by paying 3 percent for the entire transaction processing in addition to the 6-12 percent levied on travelers.

Going along with this architecture, Airbnb not only makes good money from homeowners as well as tourists, but it also fits all parties conveniently. And, what impact does that have on the rental market as a whole? Turning houses into hotels and rendering the latter partly redundant has sparked much debate among companies, advocates, citizens, lawmakers, and hospitality industry players. Airbnb not only forges those international friendships, according to proponents, but it also offers a trustworthy forum that travelers may utilize to secure decent, inexpensive accommodation. Critics, on the other hand, argue the short-term rental market has become so lucrative that greedy tenants and landlords illegally steer domestic stocks into the sector.

For example, in San Francisco, it was unlawful to rent out a property in multi-unit buildings for less than a month. The city, which surprisingly hosts Airbnb headquarters, has changed only through an ordinance passed on February 1, 2015, essentially legalizing short-term rentals. Before that, citizens of San Francisco used to take advantage of the poorly enforced prohibition to rent travelers their properties illegally. Ironically, they also now have an Office of Short-Term Rental dedicated entirely to administering and monitoring the new ordinance. It is a move that has been dramatically influenced by Airbnb's boardroom, according to critics.

The subsequent report showed that despite a decline in a portion of the properties, Airbnb rentals rose by 13.8 percent, with an average reservation price of $202 a night in shared rooms, private rooms, and whole houses, marking a 10.9 percent increase in rental prices.

In terms of individual price appreciation, wonderfully shared rooms saw a price increase of 55 percent over the 12 months to close the year at $124.

On the other hand, private homes managed only a 6% appreciation rate, rising to $123, while whole houses made significant gains of 13.3%, rising to $255 per household.

The companies analyzed comments made by legitimate visitors on individual properties listed on the Airbnb website to assess the frequency of rentals. They found that hotels still had an advantage over short-term rentals in Airbnb. Opposite to popular opinion, most of the properties, to be precise 64 percent, could scarcely attract ten reviews over 12 months. The other handful, on the other hand, who received many reports, apparently won them in clusters, thereby increasing the average number of reviews per property to 22. Entire houses, with an average number of 26 studies over the 52 weeks, proved to be the most frequented.

Previously, the New York Attorney General had done a similar analysis a year before the Chronicles report to determine the effect of Airbnb on New York Rentals. Through a report that is growing being disputed by the hotel industry, the department established that in the year 2014, about two thousand units rented out for 182 days or more.

3.3 Facilities and Length of Stay

Most of the time, the hotel industry can provide the basic needs of the rooms. These are a bed, a closet, a TV, a bathroom, and a shower. The more spacious rooms provide a seating area and a bathroom. Overall, a hotel offers no kitchen or the option to prepare and cook your meals. More often, within the hotel building, hotels provide a restaurant where guests can enjoy their breakfast, lunch, or dinner. Additionally, some hotels offer a common seating area or a conference room where business people can meet.

There are two distinct categories to define for Airbnb accommodations: apartments and full houses, or rooms. Both accommodations generally offer the same basic needs as a hotel. Still, as an individual rent the housing, guests often have the opportunity to use the kitchen and the seating area of their host, since the host should also have this at his / her disposal if the accommodation not rented out. Most of the time, the category of full houses and apartments offers an entire apartment with a bed, kitchen, seating area, and a bathroom where you will have more privacy. You will usually be given a bed and wardrobe in the room group, and you will have access to a general bathroom, seating area, and kitchen. With this option, getting in touch with the host is relatively more comfortable, and thus meeting new people.

The private rental market offers condos, houses, and rooms that typically have all the amenities an Airbnb has to offer. Because the Airbnb accommodations offer the same amenities like the private rental market listings, such places would be ideal for a prospective householder or renter. Such facilities are available for short-term hosting applicants, however. Consequently, the long-term supply of accommodations could decrease.

People are looking for long term opportunities in the private rental market. As stated, hotels and Airbnb offer short term accommodation, but the average time people stay in 9 hotels is significantly less than the length of stay in Airbnb accommodations. A tourist spends an average of 1.9 nights in an Amsterdam hotel, compared to 3.9 nights in an Airbnb accommodation Airbnb Economic Impact, this disparity may occur because an Airbnb accommodation offers the impression of a' home' setting, which gives tourists the illusion they are living like a local.

Another difference in long term accommodations is the flexibility of stays in hotels and Airbnb.

The host not connected to the guests of Hotels and Airbnb.

When your stay is over, the guests will have to leave. If the guests do not want to go, they can resolve the problem by contacting the manager or Airbnb, who will mediate with the guests.

If the hosts feel this can't resolve the matter, police involvement is an alternative. A homeowner or tenant has, however, signed a contract, which makes it impossible to change quickly between accommodations. Also, a tenant has something called rent insurance that allows them to stay on the premises as long as the lease adheres. It could be a downside for landlords, as there is no room for flexibility. When a landlord wants to rent an apartment to a tenant, he is unable to evict the tenants until they leave voluntarily, or their contract terminated. Therefore, when there are tenants, a landlord cannot sell the house — because of this, renting out your accommodation via Airbnb might be more appealing for landlords.

Most hosts initially hesitate about thinking about having a guest stay with them for more than a few days. What if he's a noisy guest? What if within the household they don't get along with other people? It's always a good thing to note that Airbnb based on a review and rating system that allows the hostess to get a pretty solid picture of their guests before accepting a booking or letting them walk through the front door.

As a host, you have the power not only to screen visitors but also to restrict their length of stay. If you're somebody who usually limits your visit to 2-3 days, why not start with a week-long trial? If that works, you can expand the terms for as long as you like–bearing in mind that there are restrictions in place in certain parts of the world for longer-term rentals.

There are several ways to attract the attention of travelers in a particular location, searching for a more extended stay. The excellent idea is to give a decent discount and make sure listed in your description of the house. It would help if you as well make sure that the space is fit for more extended stays. For instance, if someone stays in your spare room for a week, you'll need to create space for their food and beverages in your pantry and refrigerator–as well as allow them access to the kitchen to cook.

When you rent out a flat or studio room, make sure you have all the necessary amenities available. Remember, this will be your guest's s' home' for a week or two, so they'll need access to the laundry facilities and clothing hanging space. Parking plans should consider, too.

If you create a low-maintenance space that is easy for guests to take care of during their stay, chances are you'll prefer long-term reservations much more. Yeah, you might get a little less every night, but you're going to get better income security if you know you're going to have someone staying with you for three weeks and then another person waiting for a month, etc. As we have mentioned, there is also the benefit of having less housework to do when it comes to cleaning and washing. You are not going to arrange key pickups and drop-offs continually. The house rules won't have to be clarified every second day. And when it comes to your neighbors, if fewer new faces are coming in and out of your apartment daily, you are more likely to get their approval.

Longer-term bookings are also suitable for hosts enjoying traveling with time off. It will help you earn a good income for the entire period if you are outside the country - plus the security of realizing that you are living and taking care of your home while traveling.

3.4 Reputation and Trust

Renown is less critical in the private rental market than for the hotel industry or Airbnb.

When a landlord refuses to treat his tenant well, a tenant has the option to leave and complain that his landlord has the poor treatment of his tenants. It goes from mouth to mouth; there is no established forum representing where tenants can argue better than others which landlord. Also, because the demand for the rooms is higher than the supply, a landlord will find a new tenant quickly.

In the tenant-landlord relationship, trust is more important than reputation. A landlord has to believe the occupant is going to behave appropriately. Only then will the landlord accept an application from the tenant to rent the accommodation. It also works the other way around; tenants must assure the landlord will also behave properly and fulfill their obligations.

The role of trust is the key to success in the sharing economy, and particularly the relationship between trusting and trusting. There is an example of 10 stock-exchanges, where there is no human interaction. But when you lend your car, home, or tools to a stranger, that involves a social risk. Trust is the result of an agreement reached by a trustor and a trustee. The trustee is the person who takes the risk of committing to a social contract by relying on the trustee and not being sure if he or she will fulfill this. The sharing economy relies on sharing with its users, but users have to be trustworthy and, more importantly, trust each other to make an exchange. That is up to reputation and behavior.

Reputation is something that can be easily assessed but can also easily imitated where behavior is harder to fake.

The trustor wants details about the trustee to reduce the risk of engaging in an arrangement. People will even go a little further within the sharing economy. It's not just the trustee's honesty that a trustee is searching for, but also the trust value. The trustee hopes to inspire people by depending on a stranger and that they are still willing to take social risks to connect with others, and by doing so, develop new trustors. Studies have shown that we can trust people who appear to share our values and personal traits better. Through engaging in the sharing economy, we build the power to make us feel comfortable with people and interactions; otherwise, we never would have thought feasible.

For Airbnb, the owner can review by visitors and vice versa. Tourists and owners are entitled to build a solid reputation.

Credibility capital is the worth of your credibility through cultures and marketplaces, such as goals, skills, and values. Botsman argues that reliability is becoming a currency that will be higher in the 21st century than our credit history.

Reputation as a currency suggests you should trust me. We will influence our image more than our credit history and have complete control over it.

In the end, credibility capital could create a massive positive disruption about who has strength, trust, and influence. Reputation can use to buy somebody else's cooperation, even people we never knew.

Positive ratings are critical to the success of entrepreneurship and the platform for the sharing economy to work.

Platform level research show that based on their interaction with individual sellers, eBay buyers conclude the market place. Buyers with poor seller experience are less likely to get back to eBay.

For Airbnb, the same end might apply. Zervas found that staying at an Airbnb accommodation resulted in an experience of above-average levels. Compared with those on other existing sites, ratings on Airbnb are more optimistic. It means you will have to receive high ratings to thrive on sites like eBay and Airbnb, which could be the essence of success for Airbnb too.

Airbnb relies on hosts and guests to do good reviews and get along. Otherwise, people aren't eager to stay with an Airbnb host if there are no good reviews. Because when guests previously had a bad experience with a particular host, the possibility exists that one's stay could be comparable with the same host. So, hosts can put extra effort into avoiding negative reviews. For instance, rejecting guests that they deem unfit, or even deleting an accommodation and making a new one for a fresh start.

To order for a landlord to offer his accommodation on Airbnb effectively, he must invest in his credibility and behavior to gain the guest's trust. It may not be relevant for the first guests staying in his accommodation, but when his reputation is below average concerning other hosts, he may lose clients. Any guest who visits will have an opinion about the shelter and how the host treated them so that a bad review could damage future revenue. The host also has the opportunity to review his guests, though. If guests want to have other Airbnb accommodations allowed, they should behave well. At this moment, Airbnb tries to minimize social harm because when the stay is considered successful, all parties benefit. It is also a specimen of how technological advances aided Airbnb's uprising.

Where an Airbnb host can reject guests or remove lodging, a hotel has no room. We must maintain a high level and provide their visitors with excellent service.

Today hotels need to be able to respond appropriately to customer needs and maintain a high level of customer service. Otherwise, bad experience from a guest could spread and be harmful to a hotel due to technological advances and social media. The credibility of hotels is also one-sided; they cannot preliminarily determine what kind of guests they are getting. There's almost no level of trust between hotels and their guests, so there's no real link. In a shared economy, hotels must be in a position to provide services that are more reliable, consistent, broader, and safer than their future competitors.

We use state-of-the-art technology and machine learning to assess the risk of each booking before anything is verified. We perform watchlist checks internationally, and we carry out background checks on every host and guest in the US. We run health seminars at home, provide free smoke and carbon monoxide detectors, and provide essential emergency information online security cards. We use multi-factor authentication to safeguard all Airbnb accounts, requiring more verification whenever a user logs in from a new device. When you use our secure online platform, we ensure your money is covered and that your funds are always guaranteed. Plus, we will not release payment to a host until the guest is safely signed in, and you should never ask to wire money or directly pay other users. If you are, we recommend that you report that activity to us. Our customer service and trust teams are on standby 24/7, and in 11 different languages in case anything happens. We provide rebooking support, discounts, reimbursements, our Dollar Million Host Guarantee, and insurance programs all to help make things right. While we cannot remove all the risk of hosting or traveling, nor can we guarantee protection, we aim to ensure that every host and guest on Airbnb has the best experience possible.

Of our more than 25 million stays in two thousand sixteen, just 0.009 percent for visits recorded significant property damage claims reimbursed for over $1,000 under our Host Guarantee program. At that point, for more than 27 decades, you could host a new reservation every day without having to file a substantial lawsuit for property damage under our Host Guarantee. However, we are continually working to improve our network, our procedures, and our security, since one accident is still one too many.

Most people are just starting to see the importance of a trustworthy Airbnb network, and all the exposure it can provide.

Tens of millions of travelers have seen the planet as locals and not as visitors. Hundreds of thousands of hosts, mostly seniors and middle-class people, helped to meet ends, welcomed travelers to their homes, and helped their communities by supporting local businesses and promoting cultural exchange.

All of this can do because of the trust that we help people bring in each other. Trust is the sharing economy's primary currency, and it's at the heart of everything we do at Airbnb.

3.5 Prices

The accommodation price is an important feature both for the short- and long-term markets — the price set to compare the supplied quantity to the amount desired. There is, as we shall see, a massive difference between the price set for short-term demand and long-term production. The disparity occurs because when people purchase an apartment for the long term, they tend to stay there for a more extended period. They will take over the responsibility for the accommodation of the landlord or seller and ensure that they can live there for a long time, offering financial stability to the landlord, too.

Also, the landlord avoids the bother of handling the booking with long term renters, preparing the accommodation, welcoming 12 guests, and saying goodbye. A tourist or businessman will only be responsible for the shelter for about 2 to 4 days, which means that when they depart, they will think less about the condition of the housing. They could ruin the place, for example, because they feel like it and have no relationship with the host or the accommodation. So, with short-term rentals, the person who rents out their accommodation is at a higher risk. The price for short term rentals is much higher to lower the risk.

The average price to spend a night at an Amsterdam hotel in 2015 was € 154 for a two-person room. The average price of a night at an Airbnb apartment in Amsterdam is € 131 for a two-person accommodation.

The price per month for rent-seekers is considerably lower than for short term accommodation. For example, for a room in Amsterdam, students pay an average of € 425 per month. For social housing in Amsterdam, the price per month for a two-person apartment is no more than € 710. Still, the private rental sector in Amsterdam is significantly higher than anywhere else in the Netherlands. The average rent per month for private rental accommodation in Amsterdam suitable for an average of two guests is € 2,223. The void exists because the area is facing a significant shortage of private housing. Meanwhile, demand from middle-income tenants is rising.

Home-seekers are also affected by private housing shortages. Data from the Netherlands Central Bureau of Statistics indicate that the residential housing price index has risen in Amsterdam. The housing price index tracks residential house price changes. Besides, Amsterdam's housing price index is at its highest point, higher even than the peak before the 2008 credit crisis. Overall, the Netherlands housing price index isn't close to the pre-crisis end.

This rise could have induced by the capital's proliferation of Airbnb lodging. Overall, the Dutch housing price index isn't close to the pre-crisis point.

Airbnb guests can access price-filtered home listings by choosing from 4 different price ranges while searching personalized to local currency for the guest. For listings in that search, each price range represents a diverse range of the nightly price.

Airbnb determines the price range in which a listing may appear. We first look at the nightly price set by the host, and then, based on how many guests in each location take the trip and the traditional nightly rates, decide the price level that best fits the listing.

For example, if you're looking for a 4-guest listing, we may include it in a lower price range than if you're looking for the same one-guest listing as the nightly price per person is more economical for guests. Or a listing of $150 per night may appear under at a less expensive location and in $200at a more expensive place.

Our diverse community is interested in homes at all prices, so as a host, there is no incentive to be in one price range over another for your listing. You can check for similar listings in your city or neighborhood to get an idea of market prices or use the Smart Pricing feature to notify your decision on what price to set.

It means the host adjusts rates based on their gut feeling and experience. There are certain benefits here, especially if you're an experienced host.

You can, on the one hand, remain in control of your pricing, but, on the other hand, it will be time-consuming and not too precise. It is something you need to take seriously.

It is a service provided by Airbnb, and it allows hosts to set up min & max pricing. Combining these and supply and demand statistics, a recommended price for your property will come up. This feature takes into consideration the nature and location of your property, the season, demand, and other factors, according to Airbnb.

Most Airbnb hosts are not happy with it, however, as it lacks the necessary consistency. There are specialized software tools used to monitor the listing prices. The mechanism is fully automated and extremely precise.

Each of Airbnb's different pricing software uses a standard algorithm to evaluate data loads. Typically, these tools take into consideration many variables that can affect your pricing, such as seasonality, day of the week, special events, etc. Airbnb pricing automation software will not only help you improve your pricing strategy but will also change your prices every 24 hours to keep them competitive.

To sum up, Airbnb differs from hotels in providing cheaper accommodations where guests perceive a more' local' experience that allows them to feel more connected to the city they are visiting. In comparison, Airbnb establishes a close relationship between the host and his guest, while a greater distance exists between hotels and their guests.

Airbnb provides short-term accommodation concerning the private rental market, though these accommodations are also suitable for long-term hosting seekers.

Because these facilities provided through Airbnb, long term accommodation seekers do not have access to them.

It shows that Airbnb has put itself between the hotel industry and the private rental sector, and both markets have an impact.

Chapter 4: Getting into Airbnb As A Beginner and Managing Your Daily Holiday Rent

Airbnb has changed the game for travelers altogether. We no longer have to face the all too limited choice for our accommodation between a hotel or hostel. Now we have the potential to select a cute little studio, a townhouse in the hipster district of New York, apartment-and everything else in between. And we get to ourselves to have it all.

We have used countless times for Airbnb, including short weekend trips to Berlin, week-long stays in Buenos, and nearly a month in Brazil. And it's something we're going to continue to use for many future adventures. With its rapid global growth, it's now also a more feasible alternative for long-term slow travelers and has helped us out extra than once during our two-year Latin American trip. In fact, in addition to housesitting, one or two weeks in our place when we were just about all set to kill our dorm mates through no mistake of their own and had a lot of travel bored, it saved us.

While it may not come with a four-legged friend, and it's certainly not free, renting on Airbnb can often work much cheaper than a hostel or hotel, especially if there's more than one of you or you're planning to stay for over a week. Also, it is an excellent way to get out of the hotel district and into a real neighborhood, which we believe to be a fantastic thing!

Nonetheless, we agree that Airbnb can be a bit daunting for first-timers used to the versatility, comfort, and security of a hotel. And maybe a little weird. That's why we built this beginner's guide so you can understand how it works, learn from our mistakes, find the perfect room, and hopefully save some money on your next trip!

Airbnb is the perfect outlet for first-time owners of vacation rentals-it is user-friendly and very popular. Getting started with it is extremely easy too. Airbnb rental management operations are a dime a dozen though–to beat the competition, you'll have to stand out.

You can't just throw your listing up without some guidelines if you want to be successful. There's a ton of rentable properties out there, so you need to stand out. Once you start working on your listing, you need to plan your property and yourself. Choosing to list your holiday property is a great way to boost some passive income from a property you don't intend to be using all the time. Yet learning how to start an Airbnb can be much like getting a rental property that always secures a new lease.

This post will help you understand the necessary steps involved and options on Airbnb resources and maintenance if you've been struggling to meet all of your maintenance obligations and managing your daily rent. We hope that you can simplify this process and continue to maintain things successfully with minimal investment in time.

4.1 Set Up A Profile

It is the first time that you have the chance to shake hands with your guests is through your Airbnb profile.

That's where you'll offer your first impressions, and most importantly, where visitors have the first chance to thin-slice you as a potential host. This kind of personal snap judgments takes only a matter of seconds, yet they can make or break a reservation. So how can you stay safe on the better end of the spectrum of first impressions? You can, of course, create a profile of the killer.

Think of your hosting profile as your curriculum vitae: make sure that your personality shines through and that you come across your target guests like a safe investment. Even without reviews, a promising profile can win you the confidence of your potential guests, as you never know which channels some users rely most on for screening on Airbnb. As you can imagine, when people rent out their homes, they want to be pretty sure you are who you say you are. It means you'll need to go through an additional verification process once you create a profile complete with a great photo! To accepted several bookings. It is quite easy to do but would include connecting a social media account, uploading a photo ID driving license, passport, and checking the email address and phone number.

The profile picture doesn't have anything to do with what you look like; it's about the values that you express. Think of your professional headshots or profile on LinkedIn again; these images meant to convey a particular message with certain ideals, not a specific physical appearance. Your Airbnb profile photo requires its distinct approach, given such overlaps. That is why knowing the do's and the don'ts of your Airbnb pose is critical.

Do smile: nothing more than a few pearly whites symbolizes the open arms of a warm Airbnb host.

Share the Airbnb account with your significant other or any relevant family members. A family image gives off positive emotions, while it also conveys the impression of coexistence, friendship, and comfort. These are all aspects that might very well be the final push for a visitor. Well, jump the fence and spend a night.

Ensure sure the picture of your profile is transparent and of good quality. You don't want to scare guests away by portraying yourself as an ambiguous blur that doesn't even trouble to take the time to refine your physical characteristics.

Do be aware of color. Other colors, such as red, can exploit the feel-good feelings, such as respectively warmth and calmness, that your potential guests experience when they look at their profiles. In other words, there is color psychology that can be spliced into your photo to help sway reservations.

Do not include any distracting environment that drains attention away from you. Just as you target to keep your listing description clear and concise, you want to convey as little background noise as possible to who you are.

Please don't take a photograph that's so too formal; it looks fake. While you want to look sleek, your number one concern is to stay approachable and friendly–these are the most overt qualities in an excellent host.

Your photo is not your only outlet for communicating who you are, though it's the first. Fortunately, Airbnb is all about Community creativity. You get the chance to upload a 30-second video or even a custom Airbnb symbol to express yourselves and the experiences you can share as a host. Have fun with this, and it's an easy way to impress potential guests by showing them just who they're dealing with, while the time commitment offers a healthy dose of confidence to your prospects when selecting you as their host or guest.

In short, if an image is worth 1000 words, you need to choose your image as carefully as you would, say, select your bio. It is your job to keep them interested in finding a photo.

Once the decision for the big profile photograph is out of the picture, it's time to move on to the' edit profile' section where you fill in all your contact information. Make sure to plug in your phone number and email address you regularly check to avoid missing potential bookings so people can reach you. There are times when even your most secure contact points will not meet you on time.

To ensure that you never miss a later booking, you can sign up with the Airbnb profile as a service provider, and our team will ensure that your requests for reservations always addressed and that the needs of your guests. You will, of course, be kept in the loop while your chat handles all communication with guests. All private contact details kept secure and sound until booking is confirmed.

Include anything and everything' free' if applicable to you, whether it is your alma mater or any of the languages that you write or you speak. You never know; perhaps you're going to land a guest who can connect in more ways than one, and those seemingly minor specifics are just what they've sold to you. Emergency contact details don't hurt either, but that's more for your convenience. The most significant thing to remember is that apart from guest communication, your Airbnb profile is the only way you can gauge your potential guests, what kind of person, and host you are. While we can cover all communication with guests for you, you are the sole captain of the image that you promote within the Airbnb community. And again, at most, that image is received within seconds. So, take your time and design your profile to the best of your strengths, so you can say' hello' as the popular and professional host you are to the Airbnb world.

4.2 Check Out the Previous Reviews

If your favorite Airbnb has been around for a while, lots of comments from previous users should make. Write. Read.

Of course, in a sea of gleaming reviews, don't concentrate on the single lousy rating, but if lots of people say the area isn't perfect, the flat was a mess, or the host was useless, it's probably worth moving on to the next rental.

If you are a novice in Airbnb, we would recommend that your very first rental is probably one with lots of good feedback. Once you've been through the system a couple of times, you'll be more likely to let some' quirks' slide and better understand the process, but newbies may need to ease up in gently. We think that Airbnb is fantastic, and we want you to be successful for the first time!

Once you've had a pleasant stay with your guests, don't be afraid to ask for a review. While five-star reviews are naturally the most desirable, Bray emphasized that you must read and respond to all analyses to build up your "chops" hosting over time.

"Big ratings are critical to success, but you can learn much from your mistakes and other people's mistakes," Bray said. He also suggested reading reviews of similar properties to get ideas to improve your own Airbnb and to keep ahead of potential problems.

Also, you can check on your guests at Airbnb. It is a service for both visitors, who may not know whether they made an error when staying at home, as well as for other hosts. For instance, if guests have a recurring tendency to cancel confirmed reservations, you may not want to book your property for them on a weekend when you know there will be a high request from others who may be more likely actually to show up for their stay.

"Being always thinking about how to improve the experience is critical," Bray said. That holds for both you and your guests as a host.

The best reviews contain information that will assist future hosts and guests. For example, you can share with your guest, host, or their affiliates about your interactions, and guests can highlight qualities that made the stay special such as cleanliness, personal touches, or convenience.

You'll also have the choice to leave private feedback to your host or guest as part of the review process. At the same time, as the reviews have written, specific private comments are exchanged.

Especially when you're just starting, everything is a boost to confidence. While a place may seem ideal, if in general, it lacks reviews-or has a mixed bag, giving it a pass is safer-at least on your first Airbnb stays. When there are hundreds of good reviews and only one lousy apple review, it is fair to assume that this could be the person, not the place.

All hosts know that it is essential that guests receive excellent feedback on their listings. In these short reviews about guests who have booked our page, most hosts also know how important it is to be sincere and direct. Understanding how to write guest reviews on Airbnb is not a big challenge, but it can get complicated. Most Airbnb hosts advise writing a guest review, no matter what went down during the stay of the guest.

Airbnb will send a prompt to the hosts to write a review after a guest checks out. It is a snapshot of the visitor, their stay, and how our room handled. After checking out, visitors also gave this reminder to visit us and our house. You and your guest will only see your reviews on this booking after both of you have completed the analysis or 14 days later. After hosts or visitors write a summary, they will edit it up to 48 hours.

Be truthful if your review breaks Airbnb's terms of service in any way that the company can delete it to help your guests plan future Airbnb trips. Your review will also help other hosts when they receive a request from these people to create their expectations. Check Out the previous studies of the visitors to get knowledge for further bookings.

4.3 Check the Location

One of the good things about using Airbnb is having you live in a neighborhood of your choice like a local. With so many options, however, it can be challenging to know which region to choose. Do your research before you book–search the net, check out the Airbnb guides, ask friends, and post questions on message boards.

You can filter your quest in that area after you have agreed on your' hood of preference. Airbnb will never give you the right location of a list until you book, but you can typically get a pretty best idea of where your pad is with the aid of a bit of operative work and Google Earth. The listing sometimes mentions the building name or nearby landmarks, making it very easy to find.

Once done setting up a profile, you can go to the homepage and choose "List Your Space," located in the upper right corner. It will prompt you to specify space items, such as, for example, the home and room type, an apartment with one room available, as well as location and how many people you are willing to accommodate. You can set up pricing per night from there, write an overview of the room, list amenities, and add pictures.

Airbnb has a group of photographers who will come and snap professional pictures of your room, free of charge, for those lacking photography skills. Anyone with a verified email address and telephone number is eligible, though there is not always the service.

Once someone sees your space and determines to rent it out, you will have complete guest approval control.

After a particularly' exciting' stay in the Toulouse suburbs, we have learned to check carefully, and double-check the location of our future Airbnb's. Another aspect that quite significantly affects property prices is location, so if it seems too good to be true, make sure you're not in the middle of nowhere or the kind of place you shouldn't go out at night.

Another right way of assessing this is through the comments. Note, the host might say something, and you might not be aware of the no-go areas of the city as a first-time visitor to the town. Past guests in the ratings are usually pretty good at potential warning guests of this. If you have a specific reason for attending an event in the area and want to make sure the property is within walking distance or accessible for public transportation, always check with the host before you book. Finish booking anywhere near your favorite place! Not. From the sites you want to visit on your trip.

For security reasons, the exact address for the properties is often not visible until you have secured your reservation. Many will provide an approximate location, and often for points of interest or landmarks nearby.

If you are staying for a particular reason, such as attending an event in the area and want to make sure that the property is within walking distance, always ask the host before you book so that you don't even end up booking anywhere near your preferred location!

Some hosts tend to exaggerate the proximity of specific landmarks to their property in the listing too, so ask for specifics again, so you end up where you expect when the time comes!

Once you have filtered your search appropriately, you can search for listings in a particular area on a map. Just toggle the "Show Map" function in the search bar's top right corner.

If you know entirely where you'd like to be in a city, this is great. However, if you're unfamiliar with a location before you book, you'll want to do some more research on your destination. For security and privacy reasons, you won't find the exact address until you've confirmed a reservation for most listings, but Airbnb provides some extra information. Hosts need to fill out a section called "Neighborhood," so make sure to read and check all of the details here. Most of the listings have a general area map, including a public transit filter. Hosts will typically list some local coffee shops or nearby attractions in the listing, so I suggest plugging into Google Maps at one of the mentioned locations and using the street view to get a precise feel for the area.

If you still need additional location information, check the reviews for any red flags, or posting any specific concerns or questions to the host.

4.4 Communication Is Key

Good Airbnb contact with both prospective and current guests also plays a crucial role in improving the perception guests have of staying with them. Therefore, it helps you attract more reservations.

Finally, if your milestone is to become a Superhot, pay close attention to your communication with your guests. Airbnb favor hosts who respond quickly and have a response rate of at least 95 percent as part of determining eligibility for Superhot status.

The contact with prospective guests is a crucial aspect of Airbnb. Reliable contact information on your profile should make clear so visitors can easily reach you and ask any questions or issues they might have about your house. Respond as soon as possible and be approachable and friendly to your guests.

When deciding where to rate your listing when searches, Airbnb takes into account how fast you are to respond to guest inquiries, so be sure to stay up to date with any requests. For an enjoyable and profitable Airbnb experience, keeping communication open is essential. It is your opportunity to lay down the ground rules and ensure a seamless service.

As we mentioned, communicating with your host is crucial once you have your reservation sorted. Each person on Airbnb has a detailed profile page that contains useful information about themselves and their home. Hosts may also ask visitors to provide a government ID, such as a passport or driver's license, before booking their listing, and then the host has to do so in exchange. Our secure messaging service helps hosts and guests to get to know each other quickly before they question or authorize a booking. However, after each stay, guests and hosts review each other publicly, so that potential hosts and guests can see those reviews and consider them before making any decisions.

Let them know when you will come, and the best way to get in touch with you. You may well be in a country where you don't have internet, so those messages your host will send with WhatsApp on the day of your arrival will be lost in cyberspace until you hit the internet again.

Find all the essential information before embarking on your flight, train, or bus. Mobile phone number, address, how to get to the accommodation, specific entry directions-all these are essential to keeping off-line. Even without a wife, the Airbnb app has a range of these available, so make sure you download it.

If you want to check-in a little earlier in the day, or if your flight home doesn't leave until late at night, make your host aware of this beforehand.

We also found that people are quite flexible and willing to fit in with our schedule, but only when they get ahead up.

The first and most major rule to follow when it comes to Airbnb messaging is to respond promptly to all guest inquiries. You will increase the number of bookings and receive more 5-star ratings by reacting swiftly.

You should also know that before making a reservation, the average traveler is investigating and making inquiries with an average of different properties. So, if you're not around to answer a potential guest's question, they'll move on to your competitors.

Recent research found that 63 percent of hosts respond within 1 hour, meaning you need to respond faster than that to secure more reservations. Thankfully the automation of Airbnb messaging can come in handy. Using the Messaging Automation feature of vacation rental apps, you will be able to significantly reduce the amount of time it takes to send responses.

Friendly communication and prompt messaging should not end immediately upon check-in by your guests. Please prove that you are always willing to help at your property during their stay.

If any questions arise, your guests will appreciate a prompt response to their messages. Though many hosts prefer WhatsApp to connect on the go with their guests, stick instead to the Airbnb app. Communicating via Airbnb helps to ensure you protected under the terms and conditions of Airbnb.

Make sure you ask your guests to download the Airbnb app before they arrive. However, if you still prefer using WhatsApp or similar messengers, make sure that you write any critical decisions and changes on the threads of the Airbnb message to stay protected by the platform.

Follow up immediately when your guests leave to thank them for staying at your house. Let the guests know; it's been a pleasure to host them just a part of the proper Airbnb etiquette. A courteous and timely gesture like this one can help to smooth out any wrinkles that would otherwise view during their stay as an awkward moment.

At the same time, ensure that you ask them to leave you with a review. You can also let know by sending monthly newsletters that you'll keep them informed about discounts and special offers.

Remember, the guest experience starts long before your guests arrive at your property and do not stop until they depart. Through taking the necessary steps to ensure that your Airbnb messaging approach provides constructive and competent engagement with you as a host, you can significantly enhance your company credibility and your bottom line. It can also build excellent communication between the two parties.

4.5 Prepare Your Property

The property needs to structurally sound and consistent with local fire code before you start anything else. If you're all set in there, let's keep going.

Where to go? First, let's compile a list of critical areas for repair and improvement. These are items that, depending on your level of involvement, may or may not require some money. It's the stuff, too, that will make a drastic difference in the rentability of your property.

Yeah, it's a given, but it can be a little more complicated than just garbage pickup. There is no more natural way to restore a property's original beauty than power-washing. Patios, brick roads, cement fittings and driveways, vinyl siding, shingles–practically everything can wash strength. Don't overdo it and blast the holes in your house's side, you can adjust the power.

It is valid for the interior as well as the exterior. Try not to get too mad about the colors. White will always work for the interior–it gives you a sense of spaciousness. If you have to go with color, light pastels will remain within the boundaries of general expectations.

It is an aesthetic boost before anything else, but there is a little more to it. If your walls peel or crack, you'll get the impression guests don't care. That can affect their decisions when it comes to cleaning up after themselves and respectful treatment of your house.

Restoring the wooden floorboards of your property can be achieved at the cheap if you are willing to put the effort. There are many guides out there like this that will guide you through that process. The floors are the second-largest feature of the interior–restoring them will bring new life into your property.

If you have some terrible carpeting covering the walls, pull up a corner, and take a look underneath. A sheetrock knife may aid this and later to cut the whole thing out. If you have wooden floorboards down there, don't hesitate to tear the carpet off.

If it is cement, you can either arrange to put in some beautiful decorative tile floors, or put in wooden floorboards. Another choice is to rent a steam cleaner and try to use the carpet to the fullest.

There's something to keep in mind: most of the decorative floor tiling you'll find has only a thin, clear coat over it that will easily scrape and chip. If you placed tiles in a traffic-filled area, take extra care in choosing a durable alternative.

If your place is overgrown with vineyards and trees, or just bland and colorless, be careful. It's not expensive and can make a difference in a country.

A flower bed that has been freshly trimmed and edged on a lawn will probably make any property attractive. Everyone likes bird baths too.

Cockroaches, ants, ticks, and other bugs on your Airbnb rental property can be a plague. By draining any points on your property that have standing water puddles, ponds, storm drains, you can minimize the number of mosquitoes. Wherever possible, ensure proper drainage so that in the future, they will not have the opportunity to reproduce there.

Do you have a dedicated septic tank at your property? If so, do you remember the last time it had serviced? Consider it done. If feces are in the system, you do not want to mess around.

Your toilets and drains require unimpeded flow. There are a lot of liquid chemicals out there meant for this alone, but don't get carried away with it too much. They not intended for frequent use–if you keep pouring it down, they can damage your pipes and seals.

When you find that after the first use, the flow not returned, consider the possibility of physical blockage-try a right old-fashioned flange pump or buy a toilet snake. Just call a professional when it's in doubt.

Technically, this comes within the guidelines of the fire code, but it needs to repeat. Does the circuit breaker flip and shut down when you turn on the microwave while watching the television? For guests, that is a considerable inconvenience. It's usually an overloaded circuit-this is something that should only be done by a specialist.

If you're the handy type, you'll be able to unassisted check out most of this stuff. Any money you can save on this can use to upgrade the furnishings of your home.

Take a room by room approach to help turn the job into something manageable. Set every budget to be practical. Do your homework–you'll struggle to finish the room if you spend half your budget on a custom-built wooden bed frame. When you pre-price stuff out, you're going to save a lot of headaches.

4.6 Competition Analysis

Competition analysis is an assessment of the strengths and weaknesses of current and potential competitors in marketing and strategic management. This analysis provides a strategic context, both offensive and defensive, for identifying opportunities and threats.

It is where exciting things are! And, if you hate math, it's in fact where things get boring and tedious!

Unfortunately, you have to take a calculated approach if you want to make Airbnb rental management your career. You will be doing some research, making some projections, and using them to adjust your strategy. Your favorable result is on the line here, but no pressure!

There are a couple of ways you can approach this–we'll be taking a combined approach. If you live in an endless summer, you are not looking for a flat rate. You'll have a range based on the demands of seasonal holiday rental peaks.

Using an Airbnb calculator is one such way to get that info. The other is merely going on Airbnb and finding properties that suit the requirements of your own.

The latter will allow you to do a more qualitative assessment. That is, if your furnishings and services are of a far higher quality than the other similar locations in your market, you can order a higher rate and fill a void.

Location Rate Calculator-this will provide you with a general price range for the area of your property. For a more accurate scale, you can filter the results to suit the specifications of your property.

Specific Research-This is just a link to Airbnb. Watch out for your location and take a closer look at similar properties nearby. Keep in mind their chairs, services, and availabilities. Weigh all this against your own and make some changes to the rates.

If you are going above the average, leave open the possibility of backing down. It is how, in your early days, you will remain competitive and allow you to build a strong base of positive reviews.

It is not an exact science-the best you can do is come. Many untamed factors come with the management of Airbnb properties. Bookings are related to economic conditions, seasonal traffic, local competition-it's a fluctuating sector.

If we get a reasonable conservative number and handle your standards, the fair will be your definition of success. When it comes to meeting your criteria, you will be starting the market with a smaller chance of failure. You'll also have higher chances of surpassing the predicted profit margin.

For your profit calculation, here's a fundamental formula: average monthly cost–Airbnb host service fee maintenance + facilities + amenities that don't tell you anything. Sorry, doing this isn't easy–luckily, there's a free spreadsheet/calculator that will get you all sorted out.

4.7 Create the Perfect Listing

You'll find success if you've taken care of your property decor and paid close attention to the rental market on Airbnb at your place.

But before you go online, there's one more critical step ahead, so it doesn't slack yet.

Arguably the most significant piece of the puzzle here is your property listing. Potential guests can come to see the property with a standard long-term rental before making a decision. Bookings made for holiday rentals based on the listing alone. Everything that the customer sees and knows about your property is whatever you put on your listing. You absolutely must have a set of great pictures for your property before you do anything else. If you've looked after your landscaping and furnishings, this shouldn't be such a hard task. I bet you have a buddy with one if you don't have a DSLR camera.

I still don't name them. It's a very sound investment to have a professional come and take photos of your house. It might run a few hundred dollars for you, but it will help you stand out.

Your pictures are the first thing anyone can see of your house. In every booking option, they are the deciding factor. If necessary, try a local real estate photographer. Anyone experienced would know exactly which lenses to sell your property and which lighting to use. Maybe not your friend with a Canon Rebel-the best way to get them done right. The main photo shows the best features of the property. It is what the search results would first expose people to, so make it a good one. In this case, it is the room of the building - the clear title on the outside, limited to fifty letters - to finance the phrases. The title highlights some essential features: the form of home, the capability, and the appeal to the venue.

Someone looking for this property will immediately know if it fits their holiday plans.

Similar properties had been fetching as much or more after researching their location. We may presume the price is correct, with their property booked solid for the next month and a half.

The description is limited to 500 characters. It's necessary because when the page is first loaded, all the text below is hidden. Here you need to be descriptive-what makes your property unique? What are its defining characteristics?

The description of this listing highlights essential features of the property without going too far into specifics. Potential visitors will be introduced in a separate area of the page to the facilities-don't get too hung up on listing those here, mainly because they all can found at different competing properties.

If there was next door rental property with the same facilities, number of rooms and price, how would you sell yours?

The example description also makes a note of the area's major tourist attractions. Sell them like they're your own if you have popular attractions around your property.

This area of text does not have a limit on the character. Describe the most immediate surroundings and public facilities available at your property train stations, parks, gyms, etc. Note any bonus features that don't fit on your list of amenities. This listing takes the opportunity to describe the available beach equipment and a storage shed.

The seller has also made sure that its description is formatted. While Airbnb's word formatting features are limited, organized lists and line breaks can do wonders.

This host has gone beyond and beyond, ensuring that their property is flawlessly clean before guests come in. Every booking has a warm welcome, they have made sure. They have finally installed self-check-in locks for the convenience of the guests.

By placing them at the head of your profile, Airbnb rewards those efforts.

When you make the extra effort, the listing will be much more appealing.

Writing the title and description of the list is challenging, as both characters are required. With this help, at the top of the page, visitors can book the bedroom. Get the necessary information about the number, so it's best to leave it in two. Keep it catchy and concise in the description and target your target market, for example,' Romantic.' It's helpful to think of your target market in the summary description and what's important to them. So, if your property is ideal for younger people as it is in a trendy and up-and-coming city, make sure your location is also present! What is the ownership of your property and try to separate it in two words, e.g., 'Walking into a new, spacious two-minute port, is what makes your property unique and better than others, and a useful way to understand what's on your list.? If possible, try to include the USP (unique selling point) of the property in the title of the listing. For example, if lots of guests seem to love the location, you could put in the title' next to, for instance' or' steps to, you would like.' These are the excellent options for creating a complete list in the Airbnb guide for managing daily rent.

Chapter 5: What Is Airbnb SEO?

Airbnb SEO (search engine optimization) dictates how prominently the listing appears to potential guests in Airbnb searches as well in the online ads Airbnb encourages. Airbnb SEO never taught to professional hosts, and it makes a massive difference to your bottom lines.

Airbnb SEO is the analysis and application of factors within the Airbnb platform, which boost your search results. We can safely assume Google's algorithm is a standard with minor variations for most other search engines.

To boost the SEO of your Airbnb listing, you will need to understand the Airbnb algorithm, which takes all the factors into account. The Airbnb algorithm brings together the on-page and off-page Airbnb SEO into consideration. One-page SEO applies to the SEO factors within the Airbnb platform, and the elements outside of the network are off-page SEO.

Airbnb SEO is the process and research of the search exposure in the Airbnb search engine through a variety of factors: an overview of your rivals, improving your listing to competing better, and, at the same time, satisfying the internal metrics of Airbnb.

Search engines are accessible on the World Wide Web—the most common of all is Google. The definition of a comparison between two search engines is equivalent. Google uses a bot that crawls over the internet, rendering sites that it does not monitor.

On the other hand, Airbnb manages the content at its website mostly so that it is an internal search engine with many layers that they can track inside their user accounts.

Google does not suffer from any restrictions when it comes to availability, so one piece of material can be accessed an infinite number of times.

Whereas Airbnb has a limited supply of its assets, and when it is not available, a searcher cannot give a listing. Because of that, the Amazon-Airbnb analogy is a much better one.

5.1 Create and Measure Your Optimization Goals

The first step is seeing where your rivals are, and finding inside them your one "optimization target." There Are three parts for optimizing your goals:

- Find Top Earners in Your Area
- Filter Listings with Clean Rankings
- Be Sure They Are Close to You

Track the top properties in your region with the highest annual sales. Visitors traveling on Airbnb are typically looking for high-quality, authentic listings that will ideally be operated by attentive hosts who will give them memorable travel experiences.

To boost your rating on Airbnb, you need to make your listing stand out, and to do that, you need to complete will part of your listing first.

A full listing lets guests know what to expect from your room.

Make sure that you have a good description of your room and that your title and explanation are attractive, detailed, and informative. Explain clearly what makes your room special, including any facilities that you provide or rules that you have.

If you have any requirements from your guests, make sure they listed in the parts of your listing in the House Rules and House Manual.

As you might know, your images on the search results page will be your Guest's first impression of your room, so make sure you have high-quality photos on your listing. Airbnb also offers a free photography service for all hosts, so be sure to take advantage of this opportunity when it is available in your area.

For a guest, nothing is more frustrating than messaging a host and getting a response a week later or, in the worst-case scenario, to get no response at all. I know this because I frequently use Airbnb as a guest, and it happens all the time. Airbnb makes money when you make money, and they want you to be fast with your responses, and they want you to answer all your inquiries. Airbnb needs you to give your guests great experiences; booking after booking and the quantity and quality of past guest feedback can have an effect on your search results. The more you collect a lot of good feedback and get five-star ratings from visitors, the more Airbnb can promote you as a host. There's not much you can do about this one, but I have to let you know that when guests do a broad search on Airbnb, the platform will always first highlight the most famous neighborhoods or areas of any region. When you live in a renowned city that visitors love to visit, for this form of guest study, it will play to your advantage.

After you've narrowed down your area's list of high-income properties, it's time to see how "clean" their search exposure is. You want to pay attention to the features that rank consistently high in the top-level quest for cities and also in the open calendar rankings.

The excellent news is that if you are a new user, Airbnb will not throw you out to the wolves. Entering Airbnb's competitive world isn't easy, but the further listing boost. It makes perfect sense to rest well.

Airbnb desires to encourage you to keep hosting, so the right way to do that is improving the new listing. In other words, it will give your property a boost in rankings ahead of more developed listings.

When you mention your property first, you'll probably get a whirlwind of views, so make hay while the sun shines. Benefit from offering lower rates than your rivals, and building a reputation at least until you have some feedback built up anyway.

You want to work on getting excellent feedback during this time, so it's putting you in good stead. Once the boost cycle starts to wear off, you will be alone to boost your ranking.

So, when is wear off from the latest Airbnb host boost? There's no method to know for sure, but it's about two to three weeks they've suggested. More than enough time to get things kicked started!! Do not skimp on pictures, I repeat, don't skimp on photos. If there's one primary way to improve your Airbnb rating, then it's the way to get high-quality images.

Only think about it. Would a listing containing amazing photos stick more to you when you look for a property? Or would a compilation of crappy low contrast photos have taken on an old iPhone sound more prominent? Benefits from using professional photos, forty percent increase in earnings twenty-four percent higher bookings twenty-six percent higher nightly price, Better pictures attract more viewers, and more views increase the chances of having a booking. Further user activity on your listing an excellent way to improve your rating on Airbnb.

Now go and do a quick search of properties in your city. It should come as no surprise that listings with great photos rank near the top.

To be competitive in this game, you need great reviews. By this, I mean ratings from 5 stars.

I will rate this as one of the best ways to improve your score on Airbnb without fail.

Good reviews mean guests like where you're. It also ensures that potential guests will see that and increase their chances of making a reservation. That means more money for Airbnb, which means a higher ranking for you in exchange. Sounds simple, isn't it?

Guests have six areas after their stay, which they will score you on. You will measure in terms of accuracy, communication, cleanliness, location, check-in, and value.

You just have to give an accurate description of your house. I can't stress this point enough, only include it all! Good or bad, whether big or small. Getting right is so important. Maybe you have a property next to the main road with lots of traffic noise? Or is it true you don't have air conditioning? You may even have a ratty windowed old house.

Hence note these shortcomings in your collection! You might think you can scare off potential guests by including these pieces of stuff in the listing, but it will help you in the long run.

If a guest uncovers some nasty surprises during their stay, you can bet your bottom dollar in their review; they will let you know. Precise classification will help prevent this from happening.

The properties closest to you are the most relevant. If your list of high revenue generators has listings all over your city, choose the ones that are closest to you and which have the cleanest looking rankings.

As a host, you get a lot of questions from potential guests. Some are vague; others are fundamental questions that you have already answered in your collection. Over time, you'll learn to distinguish serious inquiries from casual ones.

But you have to respond quickly, no matter what the issue.

Airbnb rewards hosts who will respond within at least 24 hours to all initial inquiries. Airbnb does so by tracking response rate and response time. In the search results of Airbnb, these metrics appear on your listing and help in your ranking.

The response rate is the percentage of inquiries that you address within 24 hours. Response time is the average time you need to answer a new message. Both are measured using data from the past 30 days.

If you can't give a full response, respond with a quick, "I'm going to follow up with you early." It will stop the clock. Linking your Airbnb inbox to SMS messages on your phone also helps you stay open while you're on the move.

If you want to upgrade your Airbnb SEO, you need to maintain a 100 percent response rate to all inquiries and requests for reservations. Airbnb's search algorithm feels more confident about the accuracy of your price and dates if you keep updating your calendar continuously. Make sure that you remain active on the site by checking your daily rate, availability of timetables, or weekly Pricing.

I inform the system by making small changes to near-term prices, at least once a week. Merely signing in to Airbnb every day can also boost the search placement for your listing. As a new host, I was reluctant to allow anyone to visit my house. But the more you accept bookings, the lower you know the hosting risks are. I haven't had a single bad experience with over 300 rentals.

Fast booking is a feature of Airbnb, which helps you get more reservations. Travelers like the choice of instantly reserving a room, as they would with a hotel.

When you allow booking immediately, you'll draw more serious guests who want to secure their accommodation quickly and are happy to pay the top dollar. Fast booking means that your listing booked more often and thus increases your Airbnb score. These are some points to create and measure your optimization goals in Airbnb SEO and improve your ranking using Airbnb SEO.

5.2 Study the City and Top Leaders

Now choose listing closest to you that has a beautiful blend of high rankings and is a top earner in your area. This summary is what we term the "Target for Optimization."

From here, starting from Airbnb's perspective, we will create a list of the other competitors. It is what we call the Collection of Competitors.

It is your crucial optimization target highest earner, best-looking lists, and nearest to you and the "Similar Listings" contained inside that page. These are the hallmarks when you start typing in the Airbnb search bar. Adding words and phrases to your listing in these search suggestions is one of the quickest wins you'll get.

Airbnb is home to over 6 million holiday rental properties. Sadly, to gain enough bookings to remain profitable requires more than the right price point; it takes sophisticated SEO strategies.

Search Engine Optimization (SEO), in this case, Airbnb's method of appeasing search engines to improve the likelihood of having your property listed higher in the search results. When most people think of search engines, they always think of Google or Bing, not Airbnb; when in fact, Airbnb is only a broad search engine for finding vacation rentals. Rather than being question-based, e.g., your search query.

Which age is Airbnb? It may sound evident that your search filtered by location, availability, etc., but ensuring that your listing wholly configured for the search engines means that you need to answer all the questions that a visitor might have about the content. Use the section on listing description to answer all the questions your potential guests have about the device, the venue, and even the fun activities they may expect to do. Please go through all the amenities/essentials Airbnb lists for you and go to the shop immediately and purchase as many of them as you can.

If potential guests are looking for a location, they can filter the search to only show properties that include particular items. So, if you get lazy and don't have them, you're not going to show up. Whether you've had the best location at the lowest price doesn't matter-you have missed the booking!

Issues to be discussed in your listing Include a detailed house manual so that Airbnb knows that you are going to look after the Guest. Create a guidebook on all the stunning attractions that surround your house.

Upload 15-20 images are clearly showing the property's interior and exterior. The Airbnb algorithm strongly favors hosts who respond quickly and welcome inquiries from guests. Imagine that you are trying to book a house, and it takes the host two days even to respond. You'd probably get very frustrated and switch to another home, or give up on the Airbnb platform completely. For this reason, Airbnb expects all hosts to respond to an initial inquiry within an hour of a guest. By answering all your questions within one hour, you can increase your average conversion rate and appease the search engines.

If you're starting, we highly recommend raising your nightly rate to promote a 5-star booking entry.

When you're just getting started, the last thing you want is a comment saying your place is overpriced. Make sure you meet all standards and provide prompt and constructive feedback to any of your guests.

Try to accept more than 90% of the inquiries you receive to show Airbnb that you are inspired to take reservations and that you are eager to make the user experience of the guests as simple as possible. Airbnb focused on providing its customers with excellent skills, and if you don't fulfill the requirement, they would gladly give the bookings to someone else. Regularly checking your calendar and Pricing will show Airbnb that you are up-to-date with the availability and offer competitive prices to your guests. All property owners urged to check their schedules every single day, even if it means a few bucks in changing the price.

Airbnb understands that the more you sign in and make adjustments, the more ready you are for reservations, and the less likely you are to refuse the inquiries they send.

We have played with the in-house pricing algorithm of Smart Pricing Airbnb and found it extremely favorable for the Guest. Smart Pricing often has left thousands of dollars on the table every year. Providing visitors with inexpensive lodging is one thing, but discounting so profoundly that it impacts the bottom line is another.

We suggest using a 3rd party platform that conducts daily price optimization and adjustments to the calendar. This app also creates 10-20 percent more income for homeowners than if they were trying to manage it on their own. Airbnb is a company, and they make money when you make money, so they want you to answer all of your reservation requests as quickly as possible.

Hosts who react within an hour have a high chance of getting their listings shown at the top of the research page because they are great hosts, and Airbnb rewards this. For a guest, nothing is more frustrating than asking a host about a stay and having answer hours or days later. It's just wasting their time. They probably moved on to another listing when you finally answer.

You should install the Airbnb app on your phone to be more sensitive, as it will allow you to respond to guest requests instantly from anywhere on the planet. Like any text message, you'll get a pop-up, and you can react immediately. Within this app, you can build saved answers ready to use over and over to make life easier—popular responses such as a welcoming booking, even a prompt to write a review.

Responding to booking requests quickly in a friendly manner will show visitors that you are a welcoming host and that they are more likely to book. Remember also that having turned on Instant Booking will draw last-minute bookings and increase your response time. With so many guest choices to choose from, you need to let guests Instant Book. A Guest Welcome Book is essential to set the tone for an enjoyable stay for you. When guests know what to expect and to work, they are more likely to be at ease and relaxed in your house. It would be best if you mentioned any quirks your place might have French doors lock only when the handle is up, adding tips on local restaurants and attractions and letting them know the time and method of checking out. If a guest can't turn on the television or can't find the WIFI code, they may get irritated, and the comments may show up. Set up a clear and concise Welcome book, and with the same questions, your visitors will be less likely to give you a response. These are some useful tips for becoming the top leader of the city and increasing your knowledge about Airbnb SEO.

5.3 Optimize Your Current Listing

Did you ever wonder how you can gain more on your Airbnb listing? We want to give you useful expert advice after thorough testing and loads of analysis by giving you a checklist of the techniques used by qualified Airbnb management services. You'll be able to use these tricks to improve your listing and hold your Guest's attention on making the reservation.

You have to bear in mind before anything else: searching on Airbnb works like a funnel— there is enormous potential at the beginning, then this rapidly narrows to the point of reservation.

The milestone is to stay in the funnel, leveraging, and optimizing various factors along the way that will eventually get your listing booked. When potential guests go to Airbnb, they already have pre-selected travel dates and perfect locations in mind. So, to appear, you must meet the criteria or search filters of the potential Guest. While you may not always influence these variables, following those parameters is still beneficial. Some tips to suit the first selection stage are: It's all about position and availability; hopefully, at the right time, your flat is in the right place. Travelers prefer to go to apartments near the center of town. That is most likely where their jobs will be for business travelers. It will be easier for holidaymakers to see the sights of the city.

In this case: can you always show how easy it is to walk around from your apartment, e.g., how close are you to the subway? Are you 10meters from a bus stop? A 10-minute walk to an impressive mall? Give a whole place to show them how many it can handle. By far, most visitors are going to want to have an entire room to themselves.

They stay together as well-no breakups here. The more you can handle, the more quickly you can work for parties.

Offer comforts. Wi-Fi is a must-it's needless. Other facilities or essential items in the refrigerator could include toiletries, blow dryers, extra blankets or sheets, and food.

Give something your guests will enjoy with that little extra — we'll show you exactly how to do that later. The quality has just got to be right. Price still blends in with any filter. Make sure that you are not falling out because you are too high or doubtfully weak. This part is natural. Yet, it will also be very realistic for other hosts to try and fit those requirements. The goal is to put you on top of other assets for the next step. Everyone wants this. But how do you ensure the searchers first see you? The answer is simple — excellent customer service and regularly updated listings with full information. Remember, Airbnb's rating algorithm created solely to reward hosts who can provide a great travel experience for their guests. The happier the Guest stays with, the higher your rate. Switch on' booking immediately.' Potential guests are looking for comfort when making reservations. For this, they can obtain immediate confirmation with no time to wait.

Most specifically, it's a function that gets near top marks in Airbnb's dictionary. If not, make sure that as few bookings as possible decline. Airbnb wants all potential guests to have equal opportunities, but you have the right to go with your heart and skip the challenging guests. Even though note always-happy visitors, happy hosts.

Positive guests too benefit from prompt and timely answers. The quicker these days, as with most cases. It gets good reviews from tourist's past. It's a tab on the lifeline. Gather those great reviews! These will move up your rank and gain confidence from other potentials. There are so many ways to get excellent reviews, but here's the thing: it all boils down to meeting or exceeding! The standards of guests.

Make visitors save your flat on their wish list. An essential little trick that boosts your rank-make sure the tiny little heart is bright, and your part of their favorites to compliment good reviews. Price comes in here as before, and you should probably expect it to appear in nearly every move. Here's how you do it. But a simple tip: if' Smart pricing' is allowed, the more your price matches the' Airbnb price tips,' the better the ranking; and bonus points.

Please fill in the full listing detail. When making your listing, there are quite a few fields to complete, and Airbnb likes that when you fill in all this detail. The same is true for pictures: preferably put in 12 or more photos to show Airbnb that you are supplying your guests with great visuals of your apartment.

Make sure you put some text in all the fields— Airbnb will believe you've just written a detailed summary with excellent, useful information for the benefit of your guests.

Update your listing periodically. Airbnb is looking for this, and you can receive some thumbs up if you are actively managing it. Small little updates on price, pictures, etc. Are you with us, anyway? After that, it gets simpler. I tell you.

So now, you've persuaded them to click on your listing, and they've seen your listing specifics through. Yet look to other listings as well. How do you convince them to book theirs?

Stick to amazing but realistic pictures. Make sure to give at least a dozen high-quality ones that show the best sides, link it to what your captivating title says. Here's the deal: Visitors will judge immediately from the pictures; it gives them a' feel' of how your apartment will serve the purpose of their vacation. What do your reviews say to you? Occasionally, when guests find good feedback about things that are important to them, they may be swayed.

Certain comforts. Returning to that little extra thing: How to make your stay more comfortable. It's the little things that matter to many Learning foreign languages. It could be generally hard to pull, but even having translations in your ad text would help.

Talking about things that will make your guests feel happy and excited is always necessary to represent the emotional connection and comfort rather than physical qualities. We are on the board.

All is fine, and all we need now is to: Excellent customer service. Let them know that they can get quality value from you as well as what they get from those multiple starred hotels; this also gives you higher rankings. When you ensure that you respond to your guests promptly, you can deliver this, make sure you understand their needs.

Super hosting skills at Airbnb continue with excellent customer service. And excellent customer service also requires responding rapidly-ideally within an hour-to guest inquiry.

Be welcoming and polite, let the potential guests feel right at home. We don't need to expand on this any further. Does that seem like a steep road to success? It is not an easy matter. But there's a way for you to perfect your listing and get full bookings guaranteed without lifting a finger.

Airbnb property management services companies, will take the trouble and stress out of your host duties and help you benefit without any difficulty at all. This practical step-by-step funnel will certainly guide you on becoming a successful Airbnb host. But why not take a step forward to becoming an excellent Airbnb host and the hassle and tension along the way? Go show them how best to manage it, and get those reservations!

5.4 Promote Your Listing

You can take care of yourself by regularly customizing the foundation and replacing it with your new inventory details, simple metrics such as hospitality response time, guest satisfaction, and so on. Or you may fall back a little. You can take more control and earn some extra steps.

Side note with our tests, we've found that it helped improve rankings when a visitor remains on the listings page for longer. So, the milestone is to drive more attractions using the techniques discussed and to get them to stay on your page for a more extended period. One thing everyone should do is take advantage of Facebook ads. Not only does this give you additional views, but it also speeds up your knowledge of which definition and images work best to attract others. It is far more critical because it's the first step to get you more views. You can either tag travelers from your social media accounts using Facebook's travel ads or "retarget" visitors. You might also be reaching a much wider audience, but don't break from your aim of remaining relevant to your advertising, which Facebook likes. Applying this technique will give you the fastest possible results to optimize your image and title.

When it comes to business, you want to know if something will work the fastest or not, right? Airbnb has stated in the past that having your listing onto more Wishlist's will gradually increase exposure for your search.

Recently, Although Airbnb removed from its source code any "Wish list count" of the listings, making it a little more difficult to track whether people are returning the favor, we still believe it is part of their ranking signals. Just because we don't see it, doesn't mean that it's not yet a core part of their search algorithm.

Although it's not easy to convert anyone scrolling through Instagram or Facebook to finalize a booking with you, it's still important to generate views and create your brand for social proof. Based on how you set up your listing, you can add all of your social media users to a different Facebook list called a retargeting list and get better control of whether someone is booking your listing or not using ads.

This way, you don't just send people to Airbnb or HomeAway, etc. without any incentive of booking with you or not. Consider running a contest to raise awareness about your house. Seek to use pricing options such as a free stay, local business deals, and items specifically designed for travelers in your niche.

Such tests will often lead you to other possibilities and refresh your marketing mind with ideas. Now that you have all the resources you need to start improving your Airbnb, I encourage you to try it yourself or let us take care of it for you. Our goal is to be the most professional out there to manage this aspect of your holiday rental business by integrating data and delivering top quality rental services. Our business style has always been to share what we first learn and to offer our support if you wish.

Without email addresses, it is hard to communicate regularly with your guests and promote your Airbnb listing. So, what's the best way of getting emails?

Sadly, not all reservation sites exchange email addresses of guests when they book. While some shares that detail, Airbnb does not. But what you can do is call them after confirming their reservation, and ask them if they want to use their emails to stay in touch. You can also persuade them by saying by email that you are offering discounts for future stays. It allows you to start constructing a relationship to inspire clients to repeat themselves.

You can also collect emails by setting up a Facebook group for your house. You can establish so that when you invite visitors to join your group for their emails. Additionally, if you have in-person visitors, you can ask them to provide their emails upon check-in. That also gives you an excellent opportunity to chat and build a relationship with them.

While the optimal email frequency is guest-dependent, I would consider sending an email to past guests perhaps once a month and maybe a bit more frequently during the holiday seasons. You may contact past visitors about gifts, discounts, and sales, as well as tips, e.g., places to visit or things to go. You might have a Black Friday sale, for example, to incentivize past visitors to book again.

It's essential to avoid spamming your past guests with emails, as this is the best way to make them unsubscribe, which will make it much harder for you to transform them into repeat customers. You will seek to come from a place of "I have an offer here that I want to share with you because it could be of value to you. "While social media and email are great for attracting new visitors and keeping past guests involved, if you have outstanding hospitality, it'll only work. Great hospitality, after all, helps bring people back. Receiving repeat bookings from visitors is much easier if they have had a good experience. It also doesn't hurt if you have an exceptional guest experience; they are going to tell their friends about you.

Chapter 6: How Airbnb Benefits Communities?

Established in August 2008, and headquartered in San Francisco, California, Airbnb is a trusted community marketplace for people around the world to list, explore, and book unique lodging–online or from a smartphone.

Our business and the Airbnb group are leaders in the modern sharing economy, a trend which will be a significant part of the future economic growth of the world. Millions of micro-entrepreneurs are now motivated to use their underused assets to help make ends meet. This campaign distributes economic opportunities through various neighborhoods. It offers a reliable forum for millions of people that they can use to support their families, earn additional earning as a host, or pursue unique lodging opportunities as a guest.

More than 35 million guests on Airbnb have had a good and positive experience since 2008. We have worked hard to provide transparency and trust-promoting tools and resources, and we are glad to be a global chief in providing education to our society on these issues.

In short, Airbnb helps anybody to belong anywhere. The platform encourages outsiders to see a city as a local does and enables hosts to become ambassadors for the groups they love, using contact, payment, and trusted resources to empower users around the world.

6.1 Economics of The Sharing Economy

Trying to define precisely what the Economy of sharing is, would not do justice to the word. The sharing Economy is a continually changing economic principle.

It's the use of technology to enable the exchange of goods or services between two or more individuals, in the simplest terms.

The notion that shared parties will share interest from an underused ability or asset derived from this. This exchange of values takes place via a digital network, sharing forum, or peer-to-peer application. The sharing model is not a new idea since many rural communities thrived by bartering off the same purpose. But the management of share-based transactions has never been easier thanks to the openness of the internet and mobile devices.

Home-sharing has a range of benefits, including positive social and environmental impacts. To owners, Airbnb's economic interest is often life-changing, and it revitalizes communities as well as for small businesses.

At least three types of the economic benefits of home-sharing are categorized:

- Positive implications for customers and the tourism industry,
- Positive effects on local businesses and communities,
- Positive impacts on residents and households.

Positive implications for customers and the tourism industry:

Growth and the introduction of standard home-sharing lead to profound changes in the way people travel and experience destinations. Both patterns result in increased travel, increased spending, and interaction with different parts of a city than usually visited by tourists.

Our data shows that Airbnb draws new visitors who stay longer than typical tourists, spend more on local businesses, and because of their experience are more likely to be guests returning to the area.

Both facts effectively improve the tourism industry and create additional growth opportunities without the city requiring new investment or infrastructure.

• Thirty-five percent of Airbnb guests say that they either would not have traveled or shortened their trip without Airbnb.

• However, Airbnb guests stay 2.1 times longer on average and spend 1.8 times more than the usual visitors.

The increased travel and cost occurred when living in conventional hotels also continued to grow. Recent analyzes show that hotel occupancy rates in the United States are at their highest level in over 20 years, having climbed more than 10 percent since 2009, Airbnb was on the market for the first full year.

Positive effects on local businesses and communities:

Airbnb has not only changed how guests travel but also changed where guests stay while they visit. Airbnb guests spread the economic impact of travel to communities that have not historically enjoyed the benefits of the tourism industry by living in less concentrated neighborhoods.

• Seventy-four percent of Airbnb properties in significant cities situated outside conventional hotel districts.

• Not only do guests stay in different parts of the city, but research suggests that 42 percent of the daytime guest spending remains in the communities where they live.

That means more money invested outside the common areas of tourism-strengthening local communities and businesses. These developments in local commercial districts help hosts as well as residents who are not hosting.

Positive impacts on residents and households:

Thousands of hosts around the world have accommodated visitors in their homes since Airbnb founded in 2008. Hosting fundamentally helps hosts reach ends, holding neighborhood members amid the rising cost of living and disparity in income.

The income levels of Airbnb host mirror strictly the income distribution of Americans across the country, and the economic benefits also allow them to remain in their communities

• More than 80 percent of hosts share the home they are living in.

• Low to moderate-income households account for 52 percent of Airbnb hosts.

• A typical U.S. Airbnb host raises about $7,500 a year, helping them reach ends.

• 48% of the income earned from hosting on Airbnb used to pay regular household expenses such as rent and groceries.

• Fifty-three percent of hosts say that hosting income helped them stay home.

Airbnb hosts rely on this extra income to help pay bills and contribute to their savings, and this has also played an important role in resilience to the community.

Spending Overall economy increases:

More often than not, hotels and hostels situated in the middle of cities and towns, where guests have nearby shops and dining. In these central areas, these visitors typically stay and socialize, and do not bring as much business to other less-visited areas of the city. Holiday rentals, on the other hand, are a considerable factor attracting tourists to other parts of the city, which could benefit from this tourist income.

According to Airbnb, 74 percent of properties located outside the main hotel area. Guests invest 42 percent of the vast majority of Airbnb's outside the central hotel districts in the neighborhoods where they live. There is, then, a limpid correlation between the position of the holiday rentals and where they go out to eat, drink, etc.

As a result, we can conclude that properties like those listed on Airbnb will directly benefit the local Economy as visitors can spend this 42 percent in the city centers where there are hotels without them.

We need to look at cities like San Francisco, New York, and Paris to see examples of the positive impact Airbnb can have. San Francisco conducted a study that showed that Airbnb is generating about $56 million in local spending and creating 430 jobs in San Francisco. More than 400,000 Airbnb guests visited New York during the period 2012-2013. In one year, Airbnb generated $632 million in city economic activity, which included $105 million in outer-borough direct spending. As for Paris, more than 223,000 visitors have accommodated 10,000 hosts, renting mostly the homes in which they stay.

Service providers have more opportunity Airbnb as local Economy:

Airbnb's is also beneficial for both hosts and the guests they host at the vacation rental as well as for the economic impacts they provide.

The holiday rentals pave the way for visitors to visit fewer tourist areas, save money, and accommodate large families. According to research from Airbnb Economic Impact, 79 percent of travelers want to explore different communities, and 91 percent want to "live like a local"

Another great benefit for guests opting to rent a holiday over a hotel is quality. Compared with a hotel in the same place, Airbnb's tend to offer better value for money. Additionally, they can provide a more comprehensive price range and more easily cater for larger families than hotels do.

Airbnb reported enormous benefits for hosts in that hosting helped to meet ends for many families. Their statistics show that 52 percent of hosts have low to moderate-income, 48 percent of host income used to pay for regular household expenses such as rent and groceries, and 53 percent of households have been able to afford their own home.

Of the overall guest spending found in San Francisco for the study, $12.7 million went directly to the households of the local hosts. New York hosts see much more development in outer boroughs, which are regions that would otherwise not usually benefit from tourism spending. Nearly half of the hosts in Paris reported that they rely on Airbnb revenue to pay for household expenses. Another 20 percent of hosts say this new source of income has allowed them to pursue other professional or personal interests, helping to support a healthy, creative, and inventive community.

Local service providers, such as cleaners, benefit in many ways from the boom in the holiday rental industry. In having the option of rental holiday cleaning, these service providers can get fair pay and a broader work choice. For properties such as holiday rentals, cleaners would be limit to choosing to work for a hotel or a cleaning company making home visits. Many hotels have a fixed rate for their filters, which can be cheaper than they could receive when they visit private rentals.

Now sites such as Airbnb are common; cleaners have the option to work alone and choose the properties with which they wish to conduct business.

Filters can easily connect with holiday rental hosts in their region via sites such as Turnover to increase their clients.

It is an exciting time of development and prosperity for rented holiday hosts as well as guests. As a member of the holiday rental community, you help travelers appreciate a real neighborhood and the ability to live like a local. Such advantages go beyond the experience of tourists-they also boost the wellbeing of hosts, cleaners, and other business owners.

6.2 A Platform Built on The Community Trust

The comprehensive economic benefits are only possible thanks to the tools and resources that help our users build trust. Not only do we leverage the technologies and practices on which companies have relied for decades, but we also continue to grow new features and capabilities to support our customers.

The Team: The global Trust and Safety team at Airbnb is composed of approximately 200 professionals trained to assist our hosts and guests. The group works around the hour to help our community, while also ensuring hosts and guests have a 24/7 connection that they can access by email or telephone.

Trust and safety tools: Airbnb provide a range of devices, both online and offline, that support our community from the first time a user interacts with Airbnb until the end of a booking:

Verified ID: Verified ID ties the offline identification of a person such as a driver's license or a passport to the online profile they have developed on Airing, providing helpful information to both hosts and guests before making a reservation.

Payments Processing: Airing monitors payouts by managing payments on the Airing website. It offers significant protection against fraud and abuse by allowing Airing to refuse a refund to a host on the unusual occasion an accommodation is not as stated above. Hosts not charged until 24 hours after checking in with a visitor.

Home Safety Program: Airing works with our hosts and guests to provide best practices, tips, and resources, such as safety cards and emergency messaging, which improve our community's security. We work with experts-from local authorities to the American Red Cross-to provide information to our community that enhances preparedness and health.

The Host Guarantee: The Host Guarantee would compensate hosts at no extra cost to the hosts for up to $1,000,000 for qualifying damage to their listing properties, for each booking. That is an unprecedented level of travel industry security.

Host Protection Insurance Program: The Host Protection Insurance program provides coverage for airing hostess and, where applicable, their landlords under general commercial liability plans if a guest injured in a listing or elsewhere on the building property during a visit.

Robust profile and review systems: Thanks to comprehensive profiles and real, two-way feedback, guests and hosts can get to know each other before making a reservation. The review system allows reviews only from visitors with whom the host or guest has already booked, meaning users will benefit from actual input from those who have had real interaction with the person.

Host and Guest Messaging: Hosts and guests will connect via our platform to ask any questions that may occur about a pending trip before making a booking.

This capacity continues through the reservation, allowing continuous contact within the boundaries of the Airing website, fraud

Resolution Center: The Resolution Center will enable users to request or send money for items related to airing rentals, including requests for security deposits or demands for damages.

6.3 The Future Regulatory Environment

To continue to thrive, the sharing Economy, regulators and local communities need to formulate regulations that promote innovative new marketplaces and protect the public interest. As with other business developments, this means regulators should be wary of incumbents pushing baseless criticism that does not align with the real-life experience of millions of consumers and members of the community.

Online tools provided by platforms such as Airing today will make home-sharing more open and more available than ever. Authentic feedback, payment protection, and tools for trust and security will offer peace of mind.

Although unique licensing and registration requirements may have made sense for a full-time business bed and breakfast business, most hosts on Airing share the home they stay in on a part-time basis, and laws would represent the significant differences in those activities.

While many of the ancient laws in cities across the country have written for a very different time, many other communities have found ways to safely create home-sharing incentives for their people to support working families and their budgets.

Consider the case of San Jose, the third-largest city in California. The San City Council passed legislation in December 2014, enabling residents to share their homes, providing them with the ability to supplement their income and help pay their bills. Under the new law, short-term rentals in all zoning districts that allow for residential use permitted as a secondary use. The law does not place a limit on the number of days a host may share his or her home if the host is physically present during the stay hosted rental and a limit of 180 days on un-hosted short-term rentals when the host is not at home during the visit. The arrangement further empowers Airing to receive and pay related taxes to the city on behalf of our users, making it more convenient for the town as well as for the owner.

Cities around the world, too, are shifting. The U.K. Government introduced groundbreaking new rules earlier this year to ensure that London residents are free to share houses for up to 80 days a year without registration requirements. It helps tourists to one of the most famous cities in the world to experience it like a local and help daily people afford the rising cost of living. Response to suggestions in the independent review of the sharing economy, the U.K. Government has announced a series of measures to encourage the sharing Economy in the Chancellor's annual budget statement. London has joined a growing list of European cities, including Paris, Hamburg, and Amsterdam-that have changed their rules to allow sharing of the home.

Their experience shows that these kinds of sensible regulations can and should be repeated across the United States, meaning that people across the country can continue to benefit from the additional revenue and additional support offered by this program to their communities.

We look ahead to continuing to work with you in this changing Economy towards wise and sensible regulation that encourages increased tourism and ensures residents can rely on this opportunity to help pay their bills.

Innovations can also trigger regulatory action based on rent-seeking behavior, as rivals promote regulation and enforcement to protect their market position and hamper innovation. This maneuvering may be necessary because technologies can pose an existential threat to existing goods and companies. Umber and Lift, like Airing, are part of the sharing Economy, many of which make it suitable for regulatory tensions. Firstly, developments in the Digital Economy are focused on the rapid advancement of internet and mobile technology, making it difficult for policy-makers to keep pace. Second, several of the most common collaborative economy services exist within highly regulated industries, such as short-term accommodation from Airbnb, transportation from Uber, and finance from Prosper. Thirdly, as the CEO of Airbnb, has pointed out, the decentralized Economy has precipitated the rise of micro-entrepreneurs who question the distinction between companies and individuals. The blurring of conventional boundaries poses severe consumer protection issues, such as Will Airbnb residences follow the same safety standards as hotels? In few cases, strict regulations may even prevent the introduction of disruptive technologies since these lower goods, while' good enough' for customers, are not' good enough' to comply with existing regulatory standards. Airbnb provides an excellent example of this problem, as Airbnb residences frequently fail to meet the safety standards levied on hotels and other traditional accommodations, and Airbnb emerged simply by ignoring the current regulatory framework that would otherwise have stifled it.

Conclusion

Airbnb is a fast-growing online service, i.e., an online travel platform for a small client group that offers a worldwide link between hosts and customers searching for accommodation. The facility itself is financed by the commission paid by the hosts for the contract accommodation which amounts to 3% of the amount specified by the host and which is substantially less than the classic tourist agency commission 20-25%, and by the commission charged by the guests from 6% up to 12%.

Seeing that the younger people of today are active consumers of information technology, which is evident from the respondents ' measured indexes, the popularity of the Airbnb service is rapidly increasing. This service best characterized by its user-friendliness, search options, and lots of useful information about the host, payment method, and security. Top-rated components of this service are the ability to change the booking date, the service's accessibility, and the use of the information and communication tools used to book.

It's not clear whether Airbnb's accession will improve the capital's social welfare. The hotel industry is finding that Airbnb is becoming a more prominent player in its business, although most of the Airbnb accommodations located outside of the tourist regions. Because these areas not designed to support the rising number of tourists, this disrupts those communities.

The municipality has imposed regulations to reduce these disturbances and, at the same time, restrain the development of Airbnb. Their first regulation, the tourist tax, provides the city with the option of generating income through the sharing platform of the accommodation and could, therefore, be advantageous for the capital. People visiting tourist countries also spend more, which benefits local businesses, and eventually, even the capital city.

The number of apartments to included is Airbnb, the ownership regulation, the 60-day supervision, and the no more than four people per booking regulation are required.

Contradictory, living in hotels is becoming more expensive. The amount of Airbnb accommodation in the city could be the cause of higher rental rates and house prices, and the number of rooms available to rent-seekers could also decrease. To increase social welfare, tourist countries use the extra income produced by the tourist tax to construct new residential buildings, thereby increasing the supply of properties for long-term lodging seekers. The enforced regulations seek to limit the amount of Airbnb accommodations.

Besides, the municipality has also announced a stop to the hotel building to combat hotel development. Even though the city is trying to contain the growth of hotels and Airbnb rentals, the data show that tourism is growing like in Amsterdam. If this is the case, the Amsterdam municipality will control tourism but, at the same time, note the potential benefits that tourism brings to the town.

More research is needed to verify if tourism is on the rise with Airbnb and with which growth rate, and whether the regulations imposed to limit the amount of Airbnb accommodation are effective.

References

1.Emily, A. and Emily, A. (2020). *A beginner's guide to Airbnb – Along Dusty Roads.* [online] Along Dusty Roads. Available at: **https://www.alongdustyroads.com/posts/2016/9/9/a-beginners-guide-to-airbnb.**

2.Ftc.gov. (2020). [online] Available at: **https://www.ftc.gov/system/files/documents/public_comments/2015/05/01740-96152.pdf.**

3.Mah, K. (2020). *AIRBNB SEO: THE #1 STRATEGY to Increase Your Views, Rankings, and Booking Rates - HigherBookings.com.* [online] Higher Bookings. Available at: **https://higherbookings.com/airbnb-seo/.**

4.Whome. (2020). *Airbnb Maintenance: Guide to Easily Manage your Vacation Rental.* [online] Available at: **https://whome.pt/blog/airbnb-maintenance.**

5.Bennett, J. (2020). *The Beginner's Guide to Airbnb Rental Management | Token Press.* [online] Token Press. Available at: **https://www.tokeet.com/blog/airbnb-rental-management-guide/.**

6.Airbnb Newsroom. (2020). *Perfect Strangers: How Airbnb is building trust between hosts and guests.* [online] Available at: **https://news.airbnb.com/perfect-strangers-how-airbnb-is-building-trust-between-hosts-and-guests/.**

7.Industry, V. (2020). *3 Ways in Which Airbnb Creates Value for the Local Economy.* [online] Vacation Rental Owners Blog - Codify. Available at: **https://www.lodgify.com/blog/airbnb-local-economy/.**

8. Rental Recon. (2020). *10+ Tips to Improve Your Airbnb SEO Strategy [2020] | Rental Recon.* [online] Available at: **https://www.rentalrecon.com/airbnb-seo-strategy/.**

9. hosts? F. (2020). *Finding guests' previous reviews for hosts?* [online] Community.withairbnb.com. Available at: **https://community.withairbnb.com/t5/Hosting/Finding-guests-previous-reviews-for-hosts/td-p/734354**.

10. Economic Policy Institute. (2020). *The economic costs and benefits of Airbnb: No reason for local policymakers to let Airbnb bypass tax or regulatory obligations.* [online] Available at: **https://www.epi.org/publication/the-economic-costs-and-benefits-of-airbnb-no-reason-for-local-policymakers-to-let-airbnb-bypass-tax-or-regulatory-obligations/**.

www.ingramcontent.com/pod-product-compliance
Lightning Source LLC
Chambersburg PA
CBHW021444210526
45463CB00002B/625